The New Normal:

Tales from International School Teachers

CURATED BY MATT MINOR
AND KEVIN A. DUNCAN
on behalf of the
Children of Haiti Project

ISBN: 1544915349
ISBN-13: 978-1544915340

DEDICATION

For all the educators who have taken the leap into the unknown and for those aspiring to do so

THE TALES

INTRODUCTION

GETTING STARTED
Matt Minor

My mother-in-law has an expression she uses when people stay up too late, drink too much, and talk for hours on end about nothing in particular. Usually after a family gathering that goes into the late hours, she will greet me the next morning with a smile and say, "I heard you guys were up ´talking smart´ last night." Normally she is spot on in her sarcastic assessment of our trivial banter, but one February weekend in 2016, my buddy Dunc and I actually did "talk smart" for once. The ideas from that long balcony conversation led to the production of this book.

When I moved to Korea in 2008, one of the first friends I made was Kevin Duncan. Although we only spent two years in the same country, our friendship has developed and strengthened through hundreds of conversations in the jungles of Laos, over color-filled sunsets in rural America, and on seaside balconies overlooking the Gulf of Thailand. When I met my wife Cailin, she joined us in our love of telling stories and making each other laugh. When Cailin and I eventually left Korea, we decided to make an effort to stay in touch with some of the core people who made our experience memorable. Our group of six international educators—who are now spread out over five countries—reunite every summer in a different city. A majority of what the "Korea Crew" does is sit around and entertain one another with interesting tales of students, travel, and experiences from the previous school year. So it wasn't a totally foreign idea in February of 2016 when Dunc pitched the idea of creating a book of short stories from international teachers around the world.

By the time we finished "talking smart" on that balcón in Medellin, the goals for the book were set: to entertain, to enlighten, and to promote education. We wanted to entertain readers with intriguing stories from a collection of international teachers, to enlighten our families, friends, travelers, and prospective international school teachers by sharing what life is like for people in our profession, and to raise money to educate orphans in a country where opportunities and resources are limited.

Unlike most of our genius ideas (Me: "Let's open a beach bar near an international school so teachers can grade essays with their toes in the sand!"), this one actually had a chance. Over the course of a few hours we began to recognize personal experiences worth sharing: signing a two-year contract to live in a country we'd never visited, Dunc's roommate risking his life to save another teacher from a potentially deadly insect bite, entrusting our lives in the hands of a jungle guide who spoke a language we couldn't quite comprehend, or experiencing the loss of my father when I was 2,500 miles from home. Our idea suddenly seemed like both a source of entertainment and a free therapy session.

Our plan for this book is to give 100% of our proceeds directly to the "Children of Haiti Project" that provides an education and learning environment that all children deserve. The overseas world has given us all so much; we are excited to have a chance to give back.

Sometimes when I talk with people from home they think I am in a "travel phase" before starting my own family or that I am getting something out of my system by living abroad. 9 years since first moving overseas, I have to disagree with them. This journey has helped shape who I am now and who I will become. To quote J.R.R. Tolkien, "Not all those who wander are lost."

THE NEW NORMAL

I. MOVING OVERSEAS

THE NEW BRIDGE
Anthony van Moppes

Curiously, the windows stay sealed despite the AC not functioning. Only 10 minutes ago the arrival doors opened to a new life, country and school.

He waited with a sign, our names misspelled. Antoni. Kellie. He whisked us from the terminal into a waiting van in one clean brushstroke, an unspoken impatience on his face.

"So what do you think of Korea?" We share the same name. Sean. My middle. His American.
"It's great."

How could I describe my feelings? I've been outside the terminal for less than the duration of most commercials. The airport is still framed in the rearview mirror. What do I think? Really?

I don't think about how in two years I will have taught my first AP class with students who will be accepted the following year to Harvard, Columbia, Brown and all the other places that students label "dream" schools and have planned to graduate from since conception.

I don't think about how I will give the commencement address almost four years from now to the most celebrated class in our school's history. I'll speak about the power of pronouns and being authentic. I will have taught Ralph Waldo Emerson and Joan Didion and I'll be smarter and more confident.

I *do* think about the students I left behind. We celebrated Sequan's 21st birthday during class just two months earlier. Eugene Smith was killed over the Thanksgiving weekend some seven months ago. Derek Melendez still wanted to remove the tear tattoo from just below his eye the last time I spoke to him.

The sweat bulges on my forehead, in my armpits, on my back. It's hot. Not California, not even New York City hot, but punishing, suffocatingly hot. A different kind of hot.
The windows remain sealed.

"Can you open the windows please?"
"What did you say?"

My first experience of a communication error. There will be many more. Many, many more. I'll wake up in Suwon after a Korean baseball game in Seoul, the bus line will end and I will have slept past my stop. It will be well past midnight.
I won't know how to get back. Nobody will understand my pleas. Suji will sound like Soju, a drink here in Korea, not where you live. I'll rely on a myriad of histrionics with a taxi driver to get back home, using only the Korean couplet "not left" or the affirmative "left" to guide us. Thankfully, my Korean word base will expand by two each year.

"This is the longest bridge ever," Sean informs me. He doesn't say "ever" but that's the implication. I'll later find out that this bridge is 13.28 miles in length. Which is pretty fucking long! In another story, this bridge would be the stand-in metaphor. "What do you think about this bridge?"

I lived for more than half of my life connected on either side by the Golden Gate. I've biked the Brooklyn Bridge as a resident of Brooklyn. *This* bridge? "It's great."

A window slips open. The air rushes in, suffocates, strangles, releases, then strangles some more. Half of what is in my luggage will be discarded within 90 days. Nobody tells you to move overseas with nothing, which is actually all you need. I'll do that at one point for the new hires. But that's a lie. All of the handouts I brought will be replaced by MacBooks. The hard copy readings will be replaced by online texts. I won't need the CDs. MacBook Airs won't even have drives to play my DVDs.

We are now driving into a neighborhood, our neighborhood for the next two years, which will become six years and then 10.

"We're almost there."

There was New York City for the past five years. I think about our neighborhood, a perfect amalgamation of cafes, hipsters, tapas bars, parks, places that have happy hour specials for both food and drinks, even on Saturdays.

This new *there* is absent of those five-year staples. Tall, neutral-colored buildings, rows of them, a futuristic, dystopian-style living in the present. But what I don't realize yet is that one of these will be my home, one slim card out of the deck. And I'll miss it when I'm away. But right now, I'm away from my family, from my friends, from comfort, and from certainty.

July 21, not even 24 hours ago, was my final day in America. I cried unexpectedly as my mom walked away and down the corridor to parking garage C in San Francisco International Airport. She rode home alone in the Mazda Miata. This moment wasn't supposed to be sad; moving to San Diego, Lake Tahoe or even New York wasn't sad. The past few days spent at my parents' house was definitely not sad, a transfer stop to bridge the two worlds of Seoul and New York City. My eagerness to cross that bridge was a study of impatience. Each hour peeled away ever so slowly, each hour of repeating newscasts. My father's sage advice surfaces the same way.

"You better be careful, son. Have you thought about what you'll do if North Korea attacks?"
"Not really."
"Well you should."
My dad briefs me on North Korea nuclear ambitions, the American citizens detained there, about the new leader. His information constructed by CNN and Fox News.
I'll actually visit North Korea close to four Mays from now.

The van stops between two buildings blocking out the sun. Curiously, the AC is on now.
"We're here." Sean helps carry the soon-to-be unneeded boxes to the elevator. Kelly and I look at each other through the humid haze, soon to become a normal element of the Korean summer, which we will thankfully escape each year. The elevator rises up 11 floors. I get bitten by three mosquitoes on the short ride up. We open the door, step into our new living room, and toss bags and boxes on the floor.
"Here's your metro card and a map. There's 10,000 Won on it," Sean tells us.

The room feels exactly like the van prior to the AC functioning.

We survey the room, slightly different expressions on each of our faces.
"So, what do you think?"

After five years of living in Korea, I can finally answer Sean's question with a measure of certainty.
"It's great."

Anthony van Moppes, a native of San Rafael, California, teaches in Seongnam, South Korea. He has taught high school English for 13 years, 7 in the US and 6 in Korea.

ELECTION
Jeong Joo

I was in the middle of teaching an introductory chemistry
course, trying to explain the difference between "molarity" and
"molality." They are both units measuring concentrations of
solutions. Molarity means moles per liter and molality means
moles per kilogram. To someone not studying chemistry, there
isn't much of a difference between the two, nor is it really
relevant. However, the main issue was the way I pronounced
"molarity" and "molality." Most listeners would not be able to
differentiate between the two terms. Despite my being a fluent,
unaccented English speaker, my tongue will just not let me
forget that Korean—not English—was my first language.
When I come across words loaded with L's and R's, my tongue
simply refuses to distinguish between them. So, to save myself
from humiliation, I just wrote the definitions on the
whiteboard.

My previous five years of working in California public schools had become a pretty miserable real life version of Groundhog Day. The lunchtime staff room conversations, the angry parent phone calls, the faculty meetings about NCLB (No Child Left Behind), and the delinquent kids getting in my face all became indistinguishable and predictable daily occurrences.

In California, I did have the wonderful opportunity to teach a handful of exchange students from Japan who were outstanding in every aspect of their learning and behavior. My most recent one, Yuki from Kyushu, would consistently score in the top decile despite only having survival English skills. She was always attentive and never neglected to greet me on her way in and out of class.

Despite my L and R handicap, I applied to work for one year as a conversational English instructor in Japan with the JET (Japan Exchange and Teaching) Programme. I was placed in a public middle school. I thought the JET Programme would put me in a school full of model students like Yuki. My first two weeks in the Land of the Rising Sun consisted of attending various workshops on Japanese culture, taking a few survival Japanese language classes, and meeting some of the school board members who I would never see again. It turned out that I was the first JET of Korean, or Asian, descent to be employed by the school district.

Instead of spending valuable meeting time learning about my exact job description, I was subjected to ridiculous questions by curious and ignorant board members. Thus, I showed up to my first day of work in a suburb of Osaka, with little preparation other than a short memorized greeting in Japanese and a self-introduction slide show for my first classes.

I had assumed that the English proficiency of my Japanese partner would be at an acceptable level. However, I did not

expect my first conversation with the English teacher to go
quite like this:
"Hello sensei, nice to meet you. I'm Jeong."
"Yes."
"Um...okay...well...I was thinking for our first lesson I would
just do a self-introduction."
"Yes."
"Okay...um...what is the class learning right now?"
"Yes."
"I mean...'what'...are they learning now?"
"Yes."

I quickly realized that the Japanese English *sensei* didn't
understand a word I was saying. It would be the first of many
shocks I would experience and adjustments I would need to
make. I eventually learned to speak Japanized English to
communicate with the *senseis*. As Japanese syllables almost
never end with a consonant, I would learn to add a vowel at
the end of each. And I would soon disregard the difference
between the L's and R's as well. If I asked, 'Where is the
elevator?' I would notice a puzzled look from my Japanese
conversational partner. Thus, I soon learned to switch my own
English by Japanizing the sentence to 'We-ah izu da eh-reh-
beh-tah?'

While English is a compulsory subject from the fourth grade,
you would never know it from the deer-in-the-headlights look
from my students while I was introducing myself. I was asked
to greet each class every day with an enthusiastic "Hello class!
How is the weather?!" Only a handful of the class would
mumble with the most irritated "Ito izu ssah-nee (It is sunny)."
It didn't matter if it was pouring rain or a blizzard outside; it
was always sunny for these students. Even on my last day at
the school, a handful of students would still reply with "Nani
shabeteiru? (What is he saying?)"

I became resigned to the fact that my Osaka students would be nothing like Yuki. One kid walked out of my class during my intro presentation and ripped out a faucet in the hallway. On another day, I broke up what I thought was a balloon fight, but upon closer look discovered those balloons were blown up condoms with lubrication. After a few weeks, I learned that I had been nicknamed Kim Jong-il because of my Korean descent. And, finally, I became a victim of the common hallway prank known as *kancho,* where students poked their index fingers up a victim's anus.

I began to wonder what the hell I had signed up for. I realized that I had to take matters into my own hands. At the next opportunity, I grabbed some little fingers, bent them backwards and said in my most threatening voice, "Do that again, and I'll kill you!"

While these types of situations were quite unbelievable, I actually enjoyed the unpredictability of the job. I was glad to be in Japan, away from the repetitive monotonous daily life as a California public school teacher. I did eventually leave the JET Programme after one year, but this experience was my introduction to the world of international school teaching; I've now been overseas for a decade and have no desire to turn back.

Now, in my international school in Korea, every time I deliver my 'molarity & molality' lecture, I can't help but to reminisce about my year in Japan which, in hindsight, was the biggest turning point in my life. As I still struggle to pronounce 'moRaRity,' I chuckle thinking about the *sensei's* request for me to prepare 30 minutes of L & R word repetitions, despite my insistence that the L and R problem cannot be solved in 30 minutes. Repeat after me,
"Glass, grass!" "Grass, grass!"
"Lush, rush!" "Rush, rush!"
"Flight, fright!" "Fright, fright!"

"Fly, fry!" "Fry, fry!"
"Lead, read!" "Read, read!"

And, just for fun, I decided to include one more:

"Election!"

Jeong Joo, a native of Anaheim, California, teaches in Seongnam, South Korea. He has taught high school chemistry for 18 years, 7 in the US and 11 in South Korea.

A LEAP OF FAITH
Melacyn Turner

It was Summer 2009 when my friend and former co-worker introduced me to the possibility of teaching overseas. I had known people who moved overseas to teach, but it still wasn't a realistic option for me. I had two sons in high school and a daughter in elementary school. I told my friend that I couldn't take my boys out of their school and their city in order to move overseas for their last year or two of high school.

Fast forward to May 2011. My youngest son graduated from high school and my friend contacted me once again, asking "what are you going to do now that your son has graduated?" At that moment, I began to put things in motion by soliciting advice from my parents and children. No one in my family had ever lived in another country. There were lots of questions and concerns: "Where would you go?" "Will you be safe?" "Will you be able to return if something happens to a family member?" "Aren't you afraid of living in a foreign country all by yourself as a single woman?"

Despite the concerns, I felt a sense of calm. My overseas friends had reassured me that everything would be OK and I believed them so I embarked on the registration process for the Overseas Placement Fair at the University of Northern Iowa.

I found it odd that a small university town, far from a major airport, has been hosting schools over the last 40 years from Colombia to China in a search to find teachers. It was equally strange to me that each year thousands of teachers were willing to commit two years of their lives to a school and country they may have never seen. Whichever is the stranger, I wanted to become one of the quarter of a million teachers recruited during the UNI Fair's history.

Through the fair, we received a huge binder with a compilation of data from all of the schools that hire and have hired at the fair. I asked my middle school-aged daughter to go through the book and pick her top 10 schools/countries. Although I was the one that would be working, I wanted her to be as comfortable about the decision as I was, since it was going to be just the two of us. If she were to feel "out of place," it would be a difficult two years. It would also put a strain on our relationship and hinder my productivity as an educator.

Surprisingly, her first choice was The American School of Doha (ASD) in Qatar. I wondered how my 11-year-old chose this school in the Middle East. I soon learned that she did her research through the various school websites. She chose this school mainly because there was no school uniform requirement. She wished to be free of a dress code and she wanted something different.

I also reviewed the binder and made my own wish list—Singapore, Vietnam, and Dubai were at the top. But an international teaching job fair can take many unexpected turns. People who think they will be in Brazil suddenly accept job offers in Kuwait. It is also very competitive, especially for the schools that pay the best salaries and/or are in the most desirable locations. These schools attract the largest number of applicants, many of whom have international experience. As this was my first overseas jaunt, I knew had to be flexible. But, at the same time, I wanted my daughter to be happy.

In February 2012, I travelled to freezing Iowa along with 750+ other candidates. Despite having researched all the opportunities before arriving, it was a daunting and overwhelming experience. With our collective wish lists in hand, I began the process. Indeed, I was fortunate to get an interview with ASD but also scheduled interviews with several other schools…just in case.

During the ASD interview, I was asked why I was interested in the school. The recruiter was amazed to hear that my daughter was an active participant in the selection of future schools. He said "that's the type of student we want at our school." He invited me back for an interview early the next morning, just before my return flight back home.

I couldn't sleep more than a few winks the entire night. I tossed and turned and prayed all night. I really wanted to go to ASD. I even lamented my lack of sleep to the recruiter the next morning just before he broke the news: "We would like to offer you a contract."

Tears of joy and happiness began to roll from my eyes. I did it…my prayers were answered! I landed my very first overseas job. Not only that, it was with a highly reputable school. But most importantly, it was my daughter's first choice. She screamed in delight when she learned that I got the job.

It is now the summer of 2016 and we have just completed our 4th year living abroad. We have enjoyed ourselves tremendously. I'm so glad that my little girl from Houston was passionate about moving to a school in the desert some 8,000 miles away. I'm so thankful for friends who took the time to provide assistance and a little nudging in this process, and I'm also grateful to the recruiter in freezing Iowa who gave me a chance.

I encourage all educators to take this leap of faith, in the knowledge that it will be an extremely rewarding experience, especially for children.

Melacyn Turner, a native of Houston, Texas, teaches in Doha, Qatar. She has taught middle school science for 17 years, 12 in the US and 5 in Qatar.

CHANGE AGENT
Jake McCullough

I first met Joe while working as the librarian at a mid-sized parochial high school in the U.S. Midwest. We had just finished our first faculty orientation meeting to open the year. I was shutting down my computer and packing up for the day when he wandered toward the circulation counter, pretending to eye the magazines on display. In his mid-thirties, Joe was well-groomed and trim, wearing crisp chinos and a freshly ironed button-up.

I'd first observed him during my presentation...his negative body language was impossible to miss. With arms emphatically crossed, his chair was pushed back several feet from the back corner table, a position that bespoke Joe's role as judge, rather than member, of the assemblage. And from what I could see, his judgement was not kind.

When the meeting ended, he sat, brow furrowed, chin on chest, ruminating; Joe didn't move. After the library slowly emptied of the start-of-school buzz, he finally rose and approached the counter. I smiled and said, "You can't decide whether to run for the door or take over this place, can you?"

His head shot up, eyeing me with a mix of surprise and caution.

"What makes you say that?"

"I was watching you during the meeting. You don't have much of a poker face."

"How perspicuous of you."

"Thanks, but I think you mean perspicacious."

"No, I don't think so."

With that I raised an eyebrow and gestured toward the enormous open Webster's on a nearby lectern.

He admitted his defeat with a devilish grin and an extended hand, and thus a friendship was born.

For the remainder of the year, Joe avoided the teacher's lounge, opting instead to lunch in the glass-enclosed library conference room behind the circulation desk. He didn't make many friends in our 10 months together, much of that related to the attitude displayed from day 1, but I was glad to join him in the library fishbowl. Our daily lunch conversations began with some verbal sparring and witty repartee, but as we continued to sit there, Joe would expound on the bitterness of his recent plight.

I would console him by offering creative scenarios whereby he might wrest control of our school from the inept administration or with tales of my own subversive exploits from years gone by, including but certainly not limited to the time I got former colleague Father Salem back for undermining the efforts of Chris, our Director of Campus Ministry, who was as sincere a man as I have ever known. Fr.

Salem emptied the entire chapel of its 300 chairs, completely uninstalled and reinstalled the sound system (twice), and enlisted a team of chapel boys to spend their lunch times each day trying to locate the source of high-pitched chirping blasphemy, a random beeping device called the "Annoy-a-Tron" I strategically had planted in his sacred space.

Yes, I did that as an adult. But if you knew Father Salem, you knew he deserved it.

The levity of the stories I told Joe provided some relief to his suffering which, unlike Fr. Salem's, was undeserved. Joe's anguish actually did not originate with me or my school; it was the result of being forced to leave his dream job at a top international school. What really ate at Joe was the diagnosis that brought him back to the states turned out to be nothing but a false positive. Upon coming back, other circumstances that resulted from the move home made a return to international teaching impossible for the foreseeable future. It had been a soul-crushing causal chain for Joe. No matter what he tried, he just couldn't silence the great "What if?" constantly screaming across his mind.

At first I balked at the hyperbole with which Joe detailed his misery. How, I wondered, could leaving a job bring about such grief? It is only now, after having spent four years living abroad that I really get it: Joe wasn't forced to leave a job, he was torn from a way of life; a life so full and rich for those of a certain temperament that, once lived, makes our past lives feel prosaic and devoid of color, texture, and flavor in ways intellectual, physical, even spiritual.

While I was busy providing Joe with sarcasm therapy, he was busy convincing me—and by extension my wife—that we should begin exploring international teaching.

One evening in February, fresh off the thrill of our first interview, we had Joe and his wife over for dinner. My wife and I were ebullient over the limitless possibilities that seemed to be opening up for our family and we were full of questions about life abroad. As his wife would politely answer each question, Joe would find ways to extract himself from the conversation, engaging our kids in play or banter. Later, when we were alone on the deck working the grill I said, "This is tough for you, isn't it?"

"You have no idea."

"You know," I said, in part to needle him a bit, in part because it felt strangely true, "It's almost like you're coming back here has opened up a place for us out there."

"Jake," he said, "I think about that every day, and that's why I hate you. Now flip the burgers before you burn them, asshole."

Those next few months were tumultuous. I had decided at some point that I couldn't continue doing what I was doing, regardless of the outcome of our international job search. Without Joe, I may have never discovered the existence of this thing called "international teaching" and I would have likely frittered away at least another couple of years before extricating myself from the professional ennui I was mired in. Joe, too, had already concluded that he could not stay very long at this school and so we were searching for our out together. We consulted each other daily, giving each other shit and encouragement in equal doses. I started preparing for the LSATs with law school as a fallback plan to international teaching, the pressure of the clock intensifying as April came to a close. Joe, we figured, could suffer through one more year here while he got his exit plan solidly in place. All that changed on a Friday afternoon when Joe's year-long journey of despair was delivered a final humiliating punch to the gut.

When it was determined that a cut had to be made due to declining enrollment, our principal made his decision based on what would result in the least amount of backlash among the faculty. Joe had made all of them uncomfortable with his respect for teaching as a reputable profession, his determination to demand more of his students, and his utter and vocal disdain for apathy and incompetence. So they let him go.

The school was losing their best teacher, a begrudgingly accepted truth made embarrassingly and utterly incontrovertible when Joe's jaw-dropping AP results arrived later that summer.

The week after Joe was told his position at our school would not exist next year, my wife and I, after a whirlwind 72 hours of interviews, researching, and more interviews, suddenly had offers at two different international schools. Though I knew it weighed heavily on him, Joe provided invaluable guidance and constant vigil and support as we navigated the process. As sensitive as I was to the recent injustice that had befallen him, I needed him during those all-important days and we both knew it.

In July, after having given away almost everything we owned, my family arrived at the airport, said tearful goodbyes to our bewildered parents, and checked our bags for a flight to Asia. As I sat at our gate, watching other planes take off, my heart leapt for the thousandth time at the vast possibilities and adventures that awaited us. In a sobering moment, I thought of Joe. I took out my phone and drafted a text, then deleted it. Tried again, deleted it. I scrolled back through our recent messages: Joe had landed a better job at a better school, and I made sure to let him know about the priest scandals in that school's past; I had crushed my LSATs, and he let me know he would have scored higher; he'd found out he would be having a boy in November, and I told him I'd pray that he was healthy and better-endowed than his phallically-challenged father; the barbs seemed endless.

I imagined Joe almost precisely a year ago, his flight landing at this same airport to disembark quite possibly at this very gate, his thoughts and feelings a sharp inversion of my own: his adventure behind him, his possibilities narrowing, his professional excitement dimming. I imagined him, chin on chest, waiting at the carousel for all of his possessions, mementoes of foreign places and exciting challenges and unique experiences which would soon be gathering dust on the shelves of a two-story house in suburbia, much like the one I was leaving, constant reminders of what was.

I looked back down to my phone and scrolled past the year's worth of smart-ass banter and witty one-upmanship that concealed the love and respect we felt for each other. As our zone was called for boarding, I typed in my text, stood and looked out to the plane we were about to board, and pressed send. "Thanks, Joe."

Jake McCullough, a native of Cincinnati, Ohio, teaches in Seongnam, South Korea. He has taught high school computers and English and worked as an Ed Tech facilitator for 16 years, 12 in the US and 4 in South Korea.

RETIRE? NOT YET!
Cathy Hanley

"Is this it? We work for 25 years and then we just stay here?" I asked my husband as I was approaching my 25th year of teaching. He said, "I'm afraid so." I responded, "There must be something else!" The idea of just finishing out my career and then settling into retirement in a place where we had lived for the previous three decades was a depressing thought for me.

I loved my job as an International Baccalaureate English teacher in a rural Nova Scotia high school, but I was definitely not ready for retirement. I was looking for something else—an ADVENTURE. I was looking for an adventure.

Some Canadian friends had reached retirement age and were teaching halfway around the world in Seoul, South Korea. At first it was awesome to live vicariously through them, but I eventually stopped looking at their Facebook pages because I was so jealous of their adventures.

My husband was not a teacher, but he had the option to consider an international position with his company. We discovered that work opportunities in many countries were restricted by age caps. Dave was 59 at the time and I was 58. We knew Canada was where we would eventually retire, but it wasn't time to settle down just yet.

In 1972, I hitchhiked around Europe for four months. Often while sticking my thumb out, I remember seeing busloads of elderly people from various countries with their Tilly hats and name tags hanging from lanyards around their necks. At that moment, I promised myself I would not wait until I was their age to travel more. I would come back to Europe or venture to new places in my 20s, 30s, 40s, and 50s. I would not travel just once a decade; I wanted the travelling to be a frequent, integral part of my life. But then life got in the way. A marriage, mortgage, career, two daughters, a mom with cancer, and other family obligations.

Sure, there was some travel, but it was not the glamorous life of journeying that I had envisioned for myself while on the roads of France and Italy in 1972. And now Dave and I were within sight of the end of our careers, inching toward our *sixth* decade walking this earth. Despite the late start, now was the time to see the world.

For Dave, 'the world' ended up being Greenville, South Carolina. Not the most exotic locale, but we agreed that if I lived somewhere interesting, he would join me on all of his vacations. After hours and hours of researching online and then attending a recruiting fair for international school teachers in Toronto, I was fortunate to get a job at the school in Korea where my friends worked. I could now check their Facebook again.

After 40 years of living together, Dave and I were off to separate countries. It didn't really hit me during the 6 months that followed. It didn't even hit me during the 16 hours on 2 different flights from Nova Scotia to Korea. I was on the hour plus ride from the Incheon airport to my apartment in Bundang, a neighborhood in suburban Seoul, when I finally realized the gravity of what I had actually done. I was really here and I was staying for two years…by myself. I had never lived on my own. I went from living at home as a child, to living with friends at university, to living with Dave as a married couple.

As we travelled into Bundang, I remember being in awe of the unending sea of 30+ story apartment buildings laid out row after row after row after row. I was a little bit disappointed that they were not the typical *hanok*, traditional Korean homes, I thought everyone would live in.

Getting out of the van, it was rainy, foggy, hot, and humid. The school representatives took me into my apartment, the 30th floor of a 31 story high rise. I had some Korean money, a couch, a bed and a fridge newly stocked with milk, bread, peanut butter, and a can of tuna fish. I did not have a cell phone and the internet was not hooked up; I could not get the TV to work, and I sat there looking out the window of this small one-bedroom apartment in a city with a metropolitan area of over 20 million people. I had come from a four-bedroom home on 7.5 acres in rural Nova Scotia. Canada only had 30 million people in total and was the second largest landmass in the world. WHAT *HAD* I DONE???

Probably the scariest day of all was the next one. I had been given instructions as to where to get the bus in the morning for my first day of in-service. I spent a lot of time trying to pick out the best outfit—casual but professional. I left an hour earlier than necessary so I could look around at where I was and get my bearings. I felt exhilarated and yet, nervous. Actually, not nervous…terrified. When I exited the apartment building and the sliding doors closed behind me, the heavens opened up and it started to pour. I was too afraid to go back into my apartment because I thought I would be late for the bus. As I had no idea where I was or where the school was, catching the bus was my lifeline to reality.

I started off in the direction of the bus stop, and then just as I was rounding the corner not fifty steps from my apartment building, I slipped on the slick marble tiles around an office building, banged my head on the side of the building, and landed in a huge pile of water. OKAY that was it. So much for independence. So much for an adventure. So much for the next two years. I wanted to go home!

I was soaked, sitting on the ground while trying to be inconspicuous and worrying that I may have seriously injured my head. I picked my soggy self off the ground, the carefully chosen outfit soaked and covered in dirt, and contemplated my next move. Still too terrified to go back to my apartment, I tentatively stood up, tried to wring out my skirt as best I could, collected my internal fortitude and sloshed off to find the bus stop. I was still almost an hour early, so I walked down the street past the bus stop far enough to find shelter but still close enough that I could get back to the stop if the bus arrived. The torrential downpour continued, but eventually a big yellow KIS bus appeared.

That day it took everything I had to not let the tears come, or to call Dave and say, "I am coming to stay with you in the U.S.—forget this Korean thing." But I didn't. I truly wanted to give it a shot.

A few months later, when I was on a 2-hour hike on the trail behind the school I started to reflect on my journey up to that point. I now knew where the bus stopped in the morning. I now knew to bring my umbrella with me at all times. More importantly, I now knew that I could survive living on my own. On that hike, my colleagues (now my friends) were talking about where they had travelled or where they were going next. These were places that I had only dreamed of back in 1972, and now I was meeting people who had been there—and I was going to go to these places, too.

During my two years in Korea, I travelled to Taiwan, Japan, Nepal, Thailand, Bali, Hong Kong, Vietnam, Cambodia, and Tanzania. On many of these trips, Dave was able to join me. My time in Korea turned out to be terrific. More than terrific—it was awesome. It was EXACTLY what I was looking for. An adventure…an adventure that taught me so much about people from other cultures and so much more about myself. I also forged friendships with so many other teachers and staff from all over the world. And it didn't matter how old I was; I hung out with people both young and old. Age was not a factor because we were all in this adventure together.

Cathy Hanley, a native of Braeshore, Nova Scotia, is a retired MS/HS English teacher. After 25 years teaching in Canada, Cathy finished her career in South Korea.

THE NEW NORMAL
Cailin Minor

During my first week in Colombia, a colleague and I were on our way to the doctor's office to get a physical. We cruised along in a manner that suggested the cab driver was rehearsing for the off chance he would find himself as the getaway driver in a high-speed chase. After nearly hitting a motorist, he slammed on the brakes because we had missed our exit on the freeway. I calmly gazed out the window as the cab driver threw the car in reverse and began driving backwards against oncoming traffic to right his mistake. At this point, I noticed my new colleague with his white knuckled grip on the seat and eyes the size of a Japanese anime character.

"This isn't freaking you out?!" he commented as the color slowly drained from his face. "Oh, um, not really," I shrugged, "this is pretty normal in Thailand."

As I sat there thinking about my not-so-normal life, I reminisced how moving abroad to South Korea was my first experience shaping the new normal. I had left the suburban Midwestern life and found myself in a massive city, living in a neighborhood full of the strangest sights I had ever witnessed.

Going to the grocery store, you would often be greeted by a gigantic smiling fish head on display for all to see. The women at the grocery store, giving away samples, wore uniforms best described as bizarre cheerleading outfits with bright colors, short skirts, and ballooning knee-high socks.

My favorite job, however, was that of the person whose sole purpose was to stand next to the cart escalator and guide your shopping cart onto the moving belt that takes customers to the next floor. You would think as an independent adult, you were fully capable of pushing a cart onto a moving walkway, but if you did, you are wrong. Attempting to refuse, a mistake I committed only once, became an odd shopping cart tug-of-war and in the end, no one won.

Whether someone was a cart liaison, food sample cheerleader, or one of a hundred other odd jobs in Korea, it always seemed to involve wearing white gloves. You might fault Koreans for many things, but dirty hands was not one of them.

On the streets, it wasn't much better. It never ceased to amaze me what one could sell from the back of a small truck. I enjoyed the crab sale, where a charming toothless man sold hot steamed crabs from the bed of his truck. I never dared to eat one, but I liked to watch what sort of person would. It turns out to have been every Korean. I also loved the gutsy egg truck man who careened through the neighborhood with 500 eggs haphazardly stacked in his open bed truck. That guy was either very confident in his driving skills or still struggled with basic cause and effect scenarios. Sometimes on Saturday mornings, I would jolt awake to the sound of angry, urgent yelling drifting through the window. Is North Korea attacking? Is someone's house on fire? Nope, it's just the guy selling melons from his tiny truck.

In Korea, I met the man that is now my husband. When we moved to Thailand, the new normal kept expanding. We became car owners, first time drivers in a foreign country, 'lucky' enough to learn the ropes by driving on the left side of the road. Driving in Thailand meant sharing the road equally with cars, slow-moving pickup trucks, dogs, motorbikes, and the occasional chicken. It was a carefully choreographed dance of chaos where everyone knew the steps, but no one knew the order. No such thing as waiting until there was a safe amount of space to pass someone on the road; furthermore, traffic laws and one way streets were merely a polite suggestion. The unofficial mantra, "Do what's best for you!," trumped any official Thai traffic law. It was enough to give a new driver a heart attack.

My favorite part about driving in Thailand was the car bingo-style collection of bizarre sightings. Each day on the way to work, I hoped to spot a new scene from the car that might one-up a previous sighting. One week, it was overtaking an elephant, who was hogging the lane and going way too slow. The next week, a man and a Saint Bernard cozied up on a motorbike, sharing a scenic drive. You could also try to view a new number of family members spotted on one motorbike (I maxed at five). The daily drive was never dull.

Back in the Colombian cab, my colleague's eyes still glared wide open as the taxi driver continued weaving in and out of traffic. A few more near-misses at high speed and he'd be ready for that chase. I tried to assure my colleague that we would arrive safely and it would all work out. I continued calmly staring out the window and smiled, thinking about how even though a crazy cab ride wasn't shocking for me anymore, I still treasured the experiences that come from daily life in a foreign country. I wasn't sharing the road with elephants on my daily commute anymore, but I was excited to see what life in Colombia would bring. I was ready for the new normal.

Cailin Minor, a native of Minneapolis, Minnesota, teaches in Medellin, Colombia. She has taught elementary school for 9 years in South Korea, Thailand, and Colombia.

THE NEW NORMAL

II. ADAPTING OVERSEAS

FLUX
Colin Weaver

Becoming an international school teacher helped me become accustomed to flux and change. Prior to teaching abroad, I'd fret over any alteration to my routine and avoid it. But now I'm able to embrace change, and doing so has changed me.

Colleagues, country, curriculum: there was always something new that made me adapt. In my earlier life, I anxiously navigated changes by clinging to what was familiar. However, I learned to trust change. Which was why I wasn't concerned about leaving my teaching position in Hong Kong for a new role, in a new place, with new colleagues.

On my last day of work, I sat at my desk, packing up my resources and decided to write a note to the incoming teacher. "Dear new 5A1 teacher, Welcome to your new room…It has served me well. I'm leaving behind my paper clip collection and this Chinese calligraphy poster. p.s. Take good care of the laminated picture of Wayne Gretzky. I trust you'll know how best to display it." I placed the note in the center of the desk, hit the lights, and shut the classroom door.

THE NEW NORMAL

Five years and two moves later, I again found myself with a new position in a new school, but this time I was in a familiar location: Hong Kong.

It was a Friday evening and on my way home a group of former colleagues invited me to join them for dinner. I was actually in the mood to stay home and order in but decided to change course at the last minute to connect with these old friends. In the mix were some teachers I had never met. One introduction went like this: "So what do you teach? 5th grade, huh? I used to teach 5th grade. Wait. What classroom are you in—and how long did you say you've been working there?" I was startled to find myself in front of my replacement.

We laughed about the note I had written to her, about how I had hung the Chinese calligraphy poster upside-down, and about the Wayne Gretzky picture. My paper clip collection had been appreciated. This chance meeting continued for a long time thereafter.

In fact, now, five years later, we are married with two wonderful boys.

It's funny to think about how I wrote that note to my future wife without knowing it at the time. My adaptation to flux and change was the catalyst for our relationship. If I hadn't changed country, changed jobs, and changed course, I wouldn't have met my wife and had my children.
I've grown to appreciate the unexpected treasure of change: the more flux, the more you are open to possibilities—open to new people, new places, new experiences. Being an international teacher taught me to be friends with flux, and we've been pals ever since.

Colin Weaver, a native of Vancouver, British Columbia, teaches in Hong Kong. He has taught primary, middle school, and adult learners for 18 years, 1 in Canada and 17 in Hong Kong, South Sudan, and Thailand.

INDIAN COOL
Kimberly Russell

My husband and two sons were still back in Bombay, so I had to attend the New Parent Dinner alone. Upon arrival at the Headmaster's house, I saw a table with name tags and was smilingly given the one which was waiting for me. I stuck it to my chest and began to mingle. "Ah, so you have twins." I heard as the first set of eyes read the sticker. "No." I answered surprised. "Twins, I see." I heard again. "Noah is finishing grade nine, but, oh, he will try it again here." I realized the awkwardness of this truth and realized the sticker said Kimberly—mother of Eli grade 9, Noah grade 9. Feeling vulnerable and a bit ashamed, I decided to reword my response for the next interaction.

After the next twin comment, I offered a bit of clarification. "Noah is academically gifted; he just needs more time to become a better student." Not much better, it sounded like one of my report card comments for some unmotivated kid. I then tried this one: "He tests well, but needs to bring his grades up to the level of his testing." It sounded too desperate for approval. I think I even heard myself say, "He is on a different plane." As if he was intellectually above school. Oh dear; people still looked at me with a cocktail mix of confusion, skepticism and pity.

"Wow, twin boys." I heard at least fifteen more times. I could read their faces. If he is not bright or his grades were that bad, how did he get into this private school in Baltimore?

My misfire attempts to explain why Noah and his not-twin brother were in the same grade were so lame that I decided to simply say, "Noah is repeating ninth grade." I waited for an appropriate moment and then switched the topic to "and where do you come from?" After all, they were all new too, so everyone had their own story.

This nametag incident reminds me of just how much cooler I am since I have had Noah. Noah doesn't lie; he doesn't exaggerate. He doesn't need to prove to anyone that he knows anything more than they do. He surely does not "teacher please." He is just who he is. He is no poser.

In fact, he is so real that when someone takes a photo of him he doesn't make a cheesy smile like the rest of us. He just looks like himself, so much so that I felt I had to train his brother to put his arm around Noah in photos. This way Noah would appear a part of the surroundings, more natural and less stiff.

I always wanted everyone to look at the camera and smile— whether they were happy at that moment or not. Similarly, when the other parents asked if I had twins, I wanted to pose that perfect picture. But then I would remember the falsity of "posing" the boys and quickly change strategy.

During our six years living abroad I took many photos. Some I posed and others I just snapped. I see some pictures of Noah just looking off, mentally someplace else, and realize that I prefer the authenticity of these real moments to the ones where I yelled, "Noah, LOOK at the camera. Eli, PUT your arm around him." Maybe Noah wasn't happy to be in some of these places; maybe at that moment he was thinking a deep thought that could change the world. And there I was, yelling for him to take part in my picture and in my time—and for what…to use him on Facebook so I could try to look cool?

Needing to create an excuse for why Noah is in 9th grade again gave me a yucky feeling of trying to present myself in a different light. I was about to pose, but it just felt wrong. It was in India where I was struck by reality.

One day, commuting home from work, I saw a woman with facial tattoos, bare feet, full sari, baby on her back, and a doll-like model of the god Dhurga on top her head. She had clearly wandered into Mumbai from a thousand years ago and ended up in front of a shop in my upscale neighborhood. This shop catered to Westerners by offering necessities like marshmallows and Pringles. I am fairly certain this woman had never heard of the United States let alone most of the items inside the store. Wherever she came from, her tribal tattoos had great meaning. The god she displayed on her head helped make a blessed living for her, just as her people have done for a thousand years. Of course, I wanted to get a snap of her with one of the boys, but I didn't. I couldn't. She was not posing; she was real.

Interestingly, on the other side of the world, and a thousand years later in NYC, I saw a woman with a rat in her bikini top with piercings and facial tattoos. These actions were contrived and attention-seeking. This was the ultimate pose. You can find posers in India, too–the white trust fund girls and boys from Northern Virginia in dreadlocks, baggy pants, unshowered and unshaven, searching for enlightenment and showing the world how Indian-cool they have become. They are trying so hard to achieve the Indian-cool look that simply isn't possible in European flesh tones.

In India, I visited the rat temple in Bikaner, where rats receive offerings because they are sacred and not used for attention. I saw piercings and tattoos which signify family or marital status or Ayurvedic cures. They are not a fashion statement. After a very short time in India, I stopped taking photos of the boys with a cool Indian backdrop. It was wrong; it was contrived and culturally insensitive. Trying to create these false photos or spin why Noah is repeating ninth grade seems equally wrong.

Noah is authentic and he is in ninth grade again.

Kimberly Russell, a native of Baltimore, Maryland, teaches in Sao Paulo, Brazil. She has taught EAL or Spanish in elementary, middle school, or high school for 21 years, 14 in the US and 7 in Peru, India and Brazil.

WITHOUT MY LAST PLACE
Tara Waudby

On our third night in Kuwait, Jeff, Erica and I walked along the Gulf, blasted by a hot sea breeze. We were all new, but Jeff and Erica's friends who had lived in Kuwait told them where to get the world's best *falafel*. "Canary's," they advised.

These were the days before Google, before smartphones, before social media. We were relying on the directions from our school's orientation coordinator. En route, we meandered along the Corniche, on the other side of the sea, chatting politely as only new friends can.

Those initial conversations of expat teachers, conversations where we wander from topic to topic modestly comparing experiences, hiding our desperation for friendship under casual auras, burying deep our need for connection, are much the same as the friendship-building of my seven-year old daughter today. The primary difference, however, is that to my daughter, the insignificant topics are paramount. It truly is essential to show off a new ChapStick flavor, to whisper intimately about a new origami design, to talk only about this "right here and now" moment without thought of yesterday or tomorrow. She shows her whole self.

Canary's was a small, no-frills restaurant tucked between what I now know to be the world's best stationery store and the back alley of a McDonald's. It was simple, with shining white floors and bright fluorescent lights that stripped away any semblance of ambiance. Unfancy, clean, an uber-polite staff, and yes, the world's best *falafel*. Not only the best *falafel*, but also the best *shish taouk* and *hummus*.

Jeff, Erica and I had all arrived in Kuwait earlier in the week along with thirty other newbies from around the world. Like me, Jeff and Erica were veteran international teachers, and like me, they were thrilled with the ease of this first dinner on our own, where the food was exquisite and everyone spoke English. Even though I had grown to love Taiwan during my past five years there, it was never easy. I never fully mastered navigating the street vendors in Mandarin with their crunchy, slimy or stringy wares. Nor was the food, even with an acquired taste, quite what I loved.

Kuwait, on the other hand, felt effortless. In some ways, I felt like I was cheating. Strip away the mosques and the *dishdashas* and I could have been in my hometown of Phoenix with its wide roads, expansive suburbs, and massive strip malls and retail outlets.

It was a successful first excursion on our own and we walked home with the satisfaction of independence only expats feel past childhood. The feeling of having successfully navigated a new culture, a scattering of seeds we hope will take root, is one like my seven-year old feels when she can ride her bike to the store alone for milk and eggs—freedom.

Amongst the newbies in our cohort were several first-time overseas teachers. One group was particularly Southern and particularly loud. They peppered our bus with "Sweet Jesuses" and "Darlings" and, to me, seemed more foreign than my new home.

On the morning after our world's-best *falafel*, they were in full form, sharing their own story from the night before, an expensive taxi ride downtown to eat a real cheeseburger at The Hard Rock Cafe.

"Sweet Jesus, I was just so sick of all that small food," said the pixie-haired one from North Cackalacky, a.k.a. North Carolina, in reference to the multiple *mezzes* meals we'd had as a group of new teachers. "Honey, real American beef and a cheeseburger never tasted so good," laughed the Texan.

That morning I watched them in awe, in wonderment of how they could forego a local excursion like falafel-seeking for an American chain restaurant. Other days, I ogled their makeup and hair. They were exquisitely put together with matched accessories down to their casual flip-flops and visor caps. They showed their whole selves up front and center. I couldn't turn away.

A year on, I was still friendly with Jeff and Erica, but it was the Southerners with whom I spent most of my time. Past their brazenness, they were kind and loving, and we established a deep friendship though we never agreed upon the falafel/cheeseburger debate.

What I learned from that first dinner, and what I have carried into the next decade of international teaching, is the idea of context. No place exists without our last place. For me, Kuwait was comforting and familiar: the food, history and people were far more similar to home than what I experienced in my five years in Taiwan. For the first-time expats however, Kuwait was as foreign as Taiwan had been to me when I had first arrived. No place exists without our last.

Tara Waudby, a TCK native to Stockholm, Sweden, teaches in Al-Khobar, Saudi Arabia. She has taught English, EAL, special education, and served as an administrator for 20 years, 3 in the US and 17 in Taiwan, Kuwait and Saudi Arabia.

A TRILOGY OF THE BEST KEPT SECRETS
Christine Martin

I. BURMA and JELLO

The red and orange gelatin cups shone like little gems under the Thai sun. My job was to arrange them neatly in rows on the table, along with the gift bags prepared an hour earlier by nine strangers. Children, aged 4-14, quickly made a similar formation on the dirt floor in front of their huts. Their dusty feet, dressed in cheap plastic sandals, made an impression on me as they walked by the guests with shy smiles and soft bows. They sat on the ground and welcomed us with songs, while a portly, pleasant woman announced the reason for the visit.

Coming from Burma, the day was like any other for these children; they were far from their home, country, and families. As refugees in Chiang Dao, they experienced the same December sun as did their guests, but their reality was much different. I thought of this while handing out the colored pencils and balls we'd bought in town; it was Christmas, but these children didn't know it.

My heart warmed in this brief exchange. Knowing that I would soon return to my comfortable lodging and eventually to my comfortable home, I wondered, what would happen to these kids? What more could be done? How could my travels contribute to others, rather than to myself?

The van bumped its way back over unpaved roads. Each of us in this van, previously strangers, now friends, sat with our own thoughts. I did not miss the holiday festivities back in the States. I had no craving for gifts or lights or carols. I didn't feel an overwhelming need to be home. And I knew then—it was a luxury not to be.

II. THE BUSH YEARS

The elementary school staff room went silent. My American and Colombian colleagues looked at each other from across the room. It was 2004 and George W. Bush managed to win a second term in the U.S. Presidential office.

This time period was marked by double wars in Afghanistan and Iraq, a slow response by the federal government to the Hurricane Katrina devastation, and more. Things didn't look good "at home."

Thinking back to my departure from California in 2002, my friends, family, and even strangers indicated their strong concern when I announced my news to accept a teaching contract in Medellin, Colombia.

Their concern was not unfounded. The media had long painted a horrifying picture of Colombia as a violent, unstable, drug-driven war zone. A reign of terror, indeed, had affected the country due to the violence among the drug lords. Despite the many improvements made in the post-Pablo Escobar era, Medellin was still known as a cocaine capital. I had difficulty accepting bullet-proof cars and bodyguards that accompanied our students and a variety of other security measures throughout the country.

But these concerns soon became secondary to the wonders of the country and the warm and welcoming people. Colombia has a rich topography with mountains, valleys, rainforests, and a desert. There are magnificent places for scuba diving on Isla de Providencia, motorcycle riding on serpentine roads, and magnificent views of the Manizales' coffee country. I recall seeing baby sea turtles make their way into the sea in El Chocó, building a bonfire on the beach in Parque Tayrona, and climbing up the snowy volcano in Nevada de Ruíz.

It was in Colombia that I learned to appreciate nature, to paint, to love Spanish music, to dance salsa and tango. While world news focused its lens on Colombia's dangers and flaws, my view embraced its beauty and riches.

I learned how to keep a balanced perspective about foreign countries and compare the facts to familiar locations. Living and working in Colombia helped me learn that situations always look worse when we are unfamiliar with them. Once we experience the reality of the unknown, we no longer are afraid.

III. CAFETERIA FLASHMOB

For both teachers and students, the end of a school year is an opportunity to loosen up. There's a jittery-ness and playfulness in the air as we taste the summer vacation just around the corner.

Picture this. Nearly two hundred 3rd, 4th and 5th graders are having lunch in the cafeteria. Teachers are doing their rounds, making sure the garbage gets sorted, supervising the kids in line, and ensuring that the kids are dismissed for recess. Midway through the lunch period, the familiar chords from ABBA's Dancing Queen come out of nowhere. A group of three teachers in sunglasses clustered together and demonstrated large dance movements. A second, third and fourth group joined in. It is clear that the teachers had practiced intensely for this event.

Students looked up from their food, pointing, and giggling. "Look at Ms. Suk!" "Mr. D, what are you doing?!" The smiles and applause transformed this flashmob event into a shared and unforgettable gift. This opportunity for fun and laughter went a long way in developing strong relationships with our students.

Teaching in Korea was a joy, both professionally and personally. Koreans place a high value on education and treat teachers with respect. This trust and appreciation impacted us as educators. In addition, the top notch tech resources and facilities gave us endless opportunities to reach the highest standards while collaborating with each other.

In addition, teaching in Korea offered us conditions which made life comfortable, opportunities for travel, and also great savings potential.

Life overseas: It is the best kept secret.

Christine Martin, a native of Pasadena, California, had 18 years of teaching experience, 7 in the US and 9 overseas in Colombia, Tunisia, Korea, and Laos. She is now an interior designer and currently resides in the San Francisco Bay Area with plans for her next stint overseas.

III. LIVING OVERSEAS

A GUEST IN THE COUNTRY
Ken Turner

As soon as he made the turn, he knew. *Something's not right here.* The street was empty, too quiet even for those days. There should have been cars, a rusty red taxi or two, maybe some market women walking by with basins on their heads. *Shit.* He'd been deliberately winding his way through secluded residential areas, avoiding the main roads, but to get home, he needed to make his way along this not-quite-thoroughfare. *Nearly home, but what's going on here?* Not much longer, maybe just three or four minutes more. A quick right turn at the top of the hill, another hundred yards or so, and he could dash through the compound gate and into safety.

He should have just hunkered down at home, he knew, like most everyone else in the city—especially foreigners. But the days of tension and inactivity had been too much. The signs of trouble, the struggle to figure out what was happening: gunshots or mortar fire at night from the direction of downtown; watching from his apartment window as a mob destroyed—literally pulled down, smashing with sticks and tearing with bare hands—the billboard with the general's portrait across the street; tuning in hourly to CNN International Africa Report to check for updates from distant Atlanta about what was happening a few miles away. The endless speculation with fellow teachers in the apartment compound: would the mobs force the general's abdication? Would the army turn on him? Would the US Embassy evacuate dependents? Would the school reopen? Was the bridge to the airport still open?

But the lack of exercise had been the worst. There was a small pool in the apartment compound, true, but he had never been a swimmer. And just the thought of jogging endless laps around the cramped interior perimeter of the compound, dodging bushes and weaving around parked cars, made him tired. He had to get out, stretch his arms and legs. He knew the neighborhood, the way the streets connected, the shady stretches and the hidden paths between buildings. Things were quiet that morning, so he took his chance.

After all, he had taken plenty of chances running over the years, although it had never felt very risky. *It's such a natural thing, putting one foot down after the other, almost always in contact with the earth.* But there are potholes, curbs (that time he misjudged the curb's height and went sprawling across a sidewalk in Caracas), ditches. He loved running in the early morning dark, but he had been undone once by a low metal rail in a Guangzhou parking lot, hidden by shadow cast by a harsh streetlight. That time he had escaped with a few scrapes and a knee that ached for a month. He'd had a few missteps from loose gravel on trails in many countries, but no major accidents.

There were other chances he'd taken, what he might call cultural chances. Of course, he believed in respecting local culture, local customs, local history. He could still remember sitting, decades ago, with other new Peace Corps volunteers in the *refectoire* of a former boarding school for Belgian boys in the eastern Congo. The naïve young American volunteers were in training—linguistic, vocational, psychological—in the provincial capital. The coordinator, a veteran of the country, was saying *Remember, when you walk around this city, that less than ten years ago during the Troubles there were white mercenaries driving around in jeeps with African heads mounted on the hoods.* The immediate stillness in the room. He had never forgotten. Of course, he respected host country culture.

But somehow, when he ran he felt almost invisible. He ran in shorts—perhaps not quite respectful dress—past mosques in Lahore, past early-morning lines of Buddhist monks in Vientiane. He was a foreigner, after all, obviously engaging in sporting activity, so it would be understood, right? He ran through markets, in China, in Peru, in Ghana: so colorful, so vibrant, he loved being out with The People, and he was sorry about the jostling that sometimes happened, the stony looks he sometimes encountered. He even cruised right by the unpredictable police and soldiers (that teenager with a helmet and rifle outside a temple in Yangon, those sweating officers manning a roadblock in Accra).

Out on a run, he felt like he was in a bubble, unseen and making no waves: a stranger, moving fast, traveling light. Observing without being observed. *In* but not *of* the picture. He reached the bottom of the hill. Now just another minute or so uphill, then a right turn at the boulevard and the quick dash to the compound gate. *Wait—what's she doing?* Up ahead, at the intersection, the old woman who sold peanuts on the corner was closing up her stand, pulling a stained tarp across the battered wooden frame. Closing up in a rush. Fully closing her stand, as she did every night—but now in the middle of the afternoon. *What?* And then he saw her look down the boulevard in the direction of his gate, peering apprehensively at something hidden from him by the concrete wall on his right. She rapidly finished pulling the tarp over her stand and scuttled across the road, heading for a side street.

A squirt of adrenaline shot up his spine. He caught his breath, felt his heart skip, but kept his legs pumping rhythmically as he approached the corner at the top of the hill. *So close now, just around the corner and a little more.* Should he turn around, head back down the hill? Move close to the wall and stop at the corner to take a look? Speed up and hope he could sprint safely to the gate? And what would he see when he hit the boulevard? A jeep with soldiers? A truck full of policemen armed with truncheons, like the one he'd seen descend on the protesters who'd smashed the billboard across the street from his apartment? The truck had appeared suddenly, men jumping out and swinging their sticks before it had even come to a full stop. People shouting, screaming, vaulting over fences and fleeing down the boulevard, punctuated with the scattered white puffs of teargas canisters launched into the crowd. It was all over so fast. Fifteen minutes later, the street was silent and empty, the only evidence of what had just happened there being the dozens of abandoned flip-flops on the tarmac.

He rounded the corner at a run. *Almost there, I'm sure I can make it.* And after all, he was a guest in the country, a neutral bystander, right? This was not his country, not his struggle. Surely that was understood by everyone.

Then he saw them and immediately knew what would happen. The crowd filled the boulevard, coming toward him but still well down the street from the compound gate, his goal. Men, mostly young, angry and chanting, eyes red-rimmed and voices loud. Their chests were bare, their faces, arms, and torsos patterned with white lines and dots, designs in paint or clay. They carried branches from the forest, big sticks with the leaves still attached. He sped up and scooted through the gate just before they reached him.

But no one had given him more than a glance. Once inside the gate, he stopped and looked back as the crowd streamed by along the street. They were headed for the radio station, the Justice Ministry, or perhaps the presidential palace. He knew what would happen, but after all, he was only a guest in the country.

Ken Turner lives in Lakeland, Florida. Recently retired, Ken worked in education for 37 years, teaching high school economics, history, and English internationally for 24 years in Zaire (now Congo), Pakistan, Cote d'Ivoire, Venezuela, China, and the Dominican Republic.

THIS IS MEXICO
Hina Hashmi

Yorkshire Man (YM) and I live for our long weekends. Luckily, due to Mexico's penchant for coups, riots and general battling, there were plenty of long weekends each year—*viva la revolución!* The long weekends, known as *puentes* (bridges), gave us an opportunity to explore parts of the country too far away to manage in just 2 days. For this *puente* we decided to head down to Bahías de Huatulco, a 10 km stretch of coastline with bays backed by steep rugged mountains and 32 different white sand beaches, some of which are only accessible by boat. A heavenly getaway, especially after a grey gloomy Christmas in the UK and the cold, rainy weather back in Mexico City.

The *puente* preparations began with great promise. We were to take an overnight bus Friday night and then fly back on Monday, combining the financial savings of a bus with the speed of a flight. Pretty clever, I know! After a successful hour long expedition to the bus station to buy the one-way tickets, our subsequent internet search left us stunned: no return flights were still available. Obviously all 23 million people in Mexico City tried to book return flights from Huatulco within the past hour. For the trip to still happen, another overnight bus became our only option. Against our better judgment, we decided to give it a go: 30 hours on a bus to enjoy less than 24 in Huatalco. 30 hours, that is, if everything went smoothly.

Friday rolled around and the mammoth journey began. 3 hours in, YM began to experience all the hallmarks of serious food poisoning. Awful at any time but doubly horrendous when stuck on a bus for 12+ hours. As the night progressed YM got paler and paler; by the time we reached Huatulco he was transparent.

We staggered off the bus, blinking in the unaccustomed daylight. Though still looking like death warmed over, YM held it together well enough for us to get to the beach for some much needed sun. By Sunday morning, YM felt way better with one major exception: the fresh open wound on his leg, a result of pulling off a massive scab that marked the spot where, days earlier, his bike lost an argument with a car bumper.

Blue skies, shining sun, snorkeling in pristine waters, exploring hidden beaches, and lazing on our own private *lancha* (small motorboat)—this was exactly what the doctor ordered. Our captain added memorable entertainment, regaling us all afternoon with stories of people he knew, including himself, that had sexual relations while sporting open wounds on their legs. Turns out they all ended up with very nasty infections and almost died, surviving only because they rubbed a mixture of coconut flesh and fish scales into the wound. YM decided to take his chances and politely declined.

We left the bus station only twenty minutes behind schedule—a local miracle! YM and I began to settle in for the long return trip. Not long after departing Huatalco, the bus stopped in the middle of the main road. Engine still running, the main driver and his partner jumped out. So we waited…five minutes, ten minutes, fifteen minutes, twenty minutes. YM decided it was time to investigate. Lo and behold, he found both drivers polishing off tacos in the *taqueria* next door. The words "take the tacos to go" didn't seem to be in their vocabulary. So much for the timetable miracle!

With full bellies, our drivers hopped back in and got us back on the open road. After surviving the audible assault by terrible Hollywood films played at FULL VOLUME, we finally drifted to a short-lived sleep. The bus swerved rather excitingly onto the hard shoulder in the middle of nowhere. Thankfully no one was hurt, but our bus was done for.

Everyone disembarked and milled around on the dark highway while we waited until the next bus, already full with passengers, could take us to the nearest town. At 2:00 a.m., we began two hours straight of standing in the overcrowded aisle. It took every ounce of energy and strength to stay upright. YM's knee gave way, his wound started weeping, and I bruised my palms from hanging onto the luggage racks.

Eventually we reached the San Marcos petrol station, the rendezvous for our new bus, gratefully collapsing against one of the pumps. We then witnessed one of the most awesome sights I have ever had the privilege to experience; in fact, I humbly offer it up as the essence of Mexico.

As our coach was parked up at the bus station, fellow bus drivers from the same coach company were zooming the other way towards Huatulco. After seeing the stopped bus and stricken bodies strewn around the gas station, they abruptly stopped and jumped out to join their fellow driver. They didn't want to miss this potential drama. An important feature of Mexican culture is an overwhelming love for a community get together. If you throw in some drama…even better!

Soon, there were no less than six huge luxury coaches stopped in the middle of the highway at four in the morning. Even better, a little old lady popped out of nowhere with the ever-present plastic bucket of *tacos sudados* (sweaty tacos). These women have special radars that can sense a drama-induced gathering and naturally, you must have catering. With bent back and gnarled fingers, she set up her little taco stall. As soon as everyone was fed, she melted quietly back into the darkness.

After a good hour of taco eating and heated consultation about the drama, the new driver finally seemed to remember he had not one but two busloads of passengers patiently waiting to get moving. After saying goodbye to the other drivers, all of whom seemed totally unconcerned that their passengers had been delayed an extra hour, our driver made an announcement: the replacement bus was further away than he originally thought; we'll need to meet it quite a ways down the road. Pitifully moaning at the idea of standing for another hour, we ambled back onto the bus and assumed our positions.

The replacement bus ended up being nothing like the luxury coach we had all paid for. In fact, it looked like it had been dragged, kicking and screaming, out of retirement. The seats were more broken spring than cushion, the creaky suspension seemed to amplify every bump in the road, and the pervasive musty smell was accented with eau de chemical toilet.

Our 30-hour bus excursion turned out to be much more than we bargained for, but all was not lost. We limped back into Mexico City incredibly tired, with broken bodies and broken spirits, but safe and comforted in the knowledge that should there ever be a future drama, there will always be tacos nearby.

Hina Hashmi, a Fifer from Scotland, teaches in Istanbul, Turkey. She has taught high school science for 10 years, 3 in Scotland and 7 in Mexico and Turkey.

LEARNING TO WALTZ IN
A STATE OF EMERGENCY
Christopher Pultz

I first learned to waltz at a coming-of-age ceremony for high school graduates in Eastern Hungary. The szalagavató, as it was called, was quickly approaching, and my head teacher informed me that one of my students would ask me to dance. The waltz. And, yes, she was serious. And, no, I couldn't politely refuse. As my mom hadn't managed to squeeze ballroom dancing between schlepping us to soccer and basketball practices, it was suggested that I join the students in the school canteen for a lesson.

The teacher it turned out was a senior at the school, a student only when she wasn't busy modeling or dancing professionally. During a break from the lesson, she invited me to the center of the floor to show me the basics. My students snickered as she twice lifted my chin to match her eyes. Seeing as I was finding it difficult to then track the three-step pattern, she said, "You put your foot between my legs." My face now matching my hair color, that about ended my lessons. And sadly, it wasn't enough, as on the night of the ceremony, I stomped all over the poor debutante's feet until she politely ended the disaster with a thank you.

Despite the failure, I've thought a lot about the waltz. It's one step elsewhere and two steps in place. There's no planning involved. And though the man is supposed to lead, you hold one another so close that you basically react together. You move and recover, over and over again. In effect, the pattern fits life in Turkey to its perpendicular first letter. Nowhere was that more apparent than in the spring of 2016 during the buildup towards my summer wedding to Gamze. And having done all of the meet and greets, and just then gathering a breath in the men's room, before our first dance as a married couple, it seemed the appropriate metaphor to consider.

We'd decided to have the wedding on a boat, a cruise up and down that ancient waterway, the Bosphorus. Marriage-wise, the pressure had been off since the civil ceremony a month earlier, one so far removed from the customs at home, it had felt more like a game show. Gamze's family had sat in the studio audience, and I answered each question from the cloak-wearing host with an "Eh-vet," the simple affirmation even carrying on for an extra syllable.

Returning to the party, a buddy handed me a slender glass of rakı, a strong, milky, anise-based liqueur that the Turks called lion's milk. A Turkish idiom warns that on your first you're a kitten, the second a cat, the third a lion, and the fourth…a donkey. Still docilely feline, I'd drained half of it in one go.

I'd already made my peace with my family's absence, but it still stung when I thought about it. If the ripped bandage had been the phone call, the wound had been slowly gouged with each attack Turkey was experiencing. I argued my decision to stay in Turkey with geographical analogies. If there were a shooting in

Los Angeles, would you still go to work in New York? None of the attacks were directed at me, most were in the East, most were between the government and the PKK. Yes, there'd been attacks in the capital and even in neighborhoods alarmingly close to where I lived, close enough for me to imagine "what if" scenarios every time Gamze and I sat in a café. But the attack by ISIS at the airport ended those arguments.

"Andrew, listen. I can't let you come."

Gamze was crying next to me on the couch.

My brother, his wife, and their 6-month old daughter were supposed to accompany my mom for a three-week trip in Turkey. They would have had a week to bask on the Mediterranean before being dined to death by Gamze's mother, later experiencing the henna night in her home town before doing the wedding on the Bosphorus. The trip had been planned for months, and none of it was going to happen.

Without them there, Gamze and I had taken other steps: getting the new house in order, buying furniture with which to store her dowry, three sets of everything we didn't need but had to have. It was our third trip to IKEA the night of the Gulenist-inspired coup, a third force for Turkish authorities to contend with. I had been promised a beer if I kept my complaining to a minimum.

With a day's worth of building materials sandwiched into our rented hatchback, we pulled into the pub. I ordered a couple of tall glasses from a long-bearded barman.
"The airport is closed," said a voice behind us into her phone.
"What?" said Gamze.
I'd just taken my first sip and was wearing the well-poured head on the mustache of my beard, just starting to feel human.
"I think it's a coup."
"A coup? You're joking," said Gamze.

She phoned her brother and looked at me and my half-drained beer; she hadn't even touched hers, "Chris, we have to go."
"Will five minutes make that much difference?"
"There are tanks on the streets."
I finished hers for her, and we hit the bank machine, where the line was civil, and the corner store, where the poured-over shelves still had a few bags of broken pasta.
"There's water in beer, right?"

The State of Emergency was declared two days before the wedding. The announcement was supposed to come at 11 A.M. It came 12 hours later, and we all sat on the balcony in Afyon listening. Afyon is named for its cash crop of old: opium. At its height, it was the center of the opium trade during the Ottoman Empire. But when it made its way to the American shores, it was exploited by counter-culturists, seen as something invasive to its halcyon daze. Threatened with sanctions, Turkey scaled back its production, and America simply got its fix elsewhere.

The first time I'd visited, I sat with her father on the balcony, and he passed me a few dried opium pods that we shook like baby rattles. Overlooking Afyon's Mordor-like mountain with its ancient castle on the top, one erected by the Phrygians, and once overtaken by Tamerlane himself, it was hard to imagine how such a culture could bend to one as young as mine.

While I couldn't understand all of the words in the news report, I certainly understood the message. "Living through a coup," one of her uncles said, "is a rite of passage in Turkey."

The next morning we went to the hammam for a ritual cleaning. Ladies to one side and gentlemen to the other, a trip to the public baths was to do us all some good, perhaps we all needed the recent events scrubbed from our outer layers.

Gamze's brother and I started in the sauna, joining two middle-aged men leaned over their paunches. They asked where I was from.
"New York."
"Amerikalimisiniz?"
"Eh-vet."

Volkan took their next question and translated it for me later. "They wanted to know if you were an agent."

We laughed. I went on with the ritual, one where a man in a plaid towel scrubbed my body down on a heated hexagon in the center of the room. Slivers of natural light stood as columns in the dark. The man had just shown me how my skin had tarnished his towel, either a hint at how dirty I was or how hard he'd worked, when the proprietor peaked his head in and asked Volkan to step outside. I stayed back, lying prostrate on the slab, waiting for them to return. After a little time passed, I got up, thinking maybe something was wrong with one of the girls, maybe Gamze's mom. When I walked into the lobby, there were plain-clothes police, and I was asked to show my passport.

They weren't cruel, they weren't friendly, they were just civil servants who'd had a rough stretch answering a call from a concerned citizen, likely one of our friends from the sauna. If you see something, say something.

The henna ceremony went ahead the following day. We danced the Turkish dances to the direction of a Liberace-like emcee from Ankara. It was a bit risqué for the former opium capital, his rhinestoned outfit a nod to Turkey's own Zeki Muren. Towards the end, Gamze and I sat side by side as globs of henna were bound in both of our palms. The only thing familiar that evening was the passport Gamze insisted I keep in my coat pocket.

A week later, those henna stains had only slightly faded. I couldn't get a straight answer about their significance, so I created my own. Like the ring I'd just about gotten used to, it was to signify the permanence of our mutual devotion. And devotion required presence. And if my devotion to Gamze was to symbolically start at our wedding, then I couldn't spend the night on the phone, and I couldn't keep on with the smiling and nodding. I had to really be there. And that, in my mind, would start with our first dance. "You good?" asked a friend passing me another rakı. I silently counted. This would be the third.

But a lion was good. It sounded even better in Turkish: Aslan.

I ascended the stairs and met my wife in the middle. The air was cool, and my eyes adjusted to the deck lights and the wavering luminescence along the Bosphorus shore, shores traversed by Jason and his ill-fated Argonautical adventure, shores I'd read as abstractions in history class. My feet adjusted to the boat's gentle sway, and as the first hard note of Sinatra's "Fly me to the Moon" sounded, the song we'd decided on during the drive over, we joined our henna-stained hands and took the first step together.

There was nobody on the boat except her, until a phone was thrust in my face with my shirtless brother clutching his 6-month old with his wife at his shoulder, and my mom in tears in the background. I held back my own tears, as there'd be time later, and instead pointed once to the screen, before turning back to my wife. We simply took the next step elsewhere, recovering soon afterwards with two more steps from where the first had taken us, and continued that way throughout the night, ever navigating the Bosphorus's unexpected sway, and the swells that will surely continue thereafter.

Christopher Pultz, a native of Massapequa, New York, teaches in Istanbul, Turkey. He has taught Language and Literature for 16 years, 6 in the US and 10 in Madagascar, Hungary, Belarus, and Turkey.

BUYING A CAR IN CARACAS
Jess Barga

The bureaucratic logistics of acquiring a car seem to me prohibitively daunting anywhere on earth, let alone the Socialist Republic of Hugolandia (a.k.a. Venezuela) circa 2010. Yet somehow, I have managed to be the legal owner of a whole motorcade of proud vehicles, from a sweat-scented '80 Monte Carlo, previously owned by a teenage wrestler, to a brakeless '85 turbo Volvo, purchased from a mustachioed scammer in a Hawaiian shirt, to a mid-decay '88 Civic purpose-bought for a Baja, CA road trip (in that mold sporatorium, radiator issues required that the heat be left on at all times, ideal for the chilly climate of coastal Mexico in July). If your background is similar to mine (middle American, middle-middle class), maybe your automotive history boasts a comparable parade? But only if you take a deep and irrational pride in your rust-encrusted Omni or your dented Corolla can we call ourselves kindred spirits. Although I recognize the ecological malice and egocentrism in this, my most American predilection, I adore having my own car, and driving it, regardless of its pedigree.

When my husband Chris and I moved to Caracas in 2010, the place hit me straight in the gut. Never mind the obvious thrill of living in a city the name of which you've probably never heard minus the appellation "murder capital of the world"— the place was brimming with character. Crystal blue sky, throbbing reggaetón, hot dog-meets-malta-meets-four-cents-a-gallon-gasoline-scent in the air...all of this with the backdrop of the verdant Avila mountain, frosted with gauzy white clouds or punctuated by a scarlet and emerald macaw gliding by on the breeze. In terms of variety and charisma, the roads themselves were a singular delight, and the most salient Venezuelan delicacies were the Lada Niva (miniature Russian 4x4, "always half broken but never broken down"), the Chevrolet Wagon R (minimalist hatchback, at once button-cute and businesslike) and best of all, the ubiquitous woody Wagoneer.

I've always been relatively heterosexual when it comes to cars. The stiff, trim lines of an 80's Civic hatchback please me to no end, and BMW's boyish hipster 2002 has been known to provoke a squeal of delight, as has the lanky but virile sumptuosity of a 70s Caddy Eldorado. But occasionally, a more feminine set of wheels will cause my head to turn (PT Cruiser, anyone?). This may be because the car that deflowered me at 16—my very first vehicular love—was a wrong-side-of-the-tracks copper '77 Thunderbird called Julio: masculine in a decidedly Latin way, but curvaceous and comely in a manner that suggested a mature, voluptuous older woman; a car less confused about its identity than perfectly content with its subtle hermaphroditic tendencies. At any rate, the girlish original model Wagoneer—bouncy, ample-bottomed, and banded immodestly with a halter top of wood-look appliqué— is my favorite car. The disproportionately frequent Wagoneer sightings in Caracas were a revelation to me, especially after living in South Korea, where it seemed that by law, all cars must be grey, black or white and unsentimentally discarded after three years of use. Plus, public transportation in Venezuela was a risky, complex riddle and taxis were just as unsafe, giving me an excuse to start browsing, even in an economy where used cars were as scandalously overpriced as gasoline was cheap. Could it be that I would finally have the chance to own my dream car—my woody Wagoneer?

I should clarify. My taste in cars runs directly contrary to my ability to fix, maintain, or even understand an engine. I once helped my dad change the oil in my Volvo, and we may or may not have had to visit Jiffy Lube afterwards with our tails hanging sheepishly between our legs. (OK, I exaggerate: my father is no mechanical moron but, unequivocally, I am.) Any sensible consumer with my boundless ignorance would have taken our well-meaning colleagues up on their offer of a reasonably-priced nondescript 2003 Chevy sedan. Why spend time searching when a good deal is staring you in the face? Better judgment not being my strong suit, I began to visit TuCarro.com obsessively instead. I dragged reluctant, infinitely sensible Chris to a sketchy neighborhood to test drive a dirt-brown Isuzu Caribe. Its incredulous, shirtless owner clearly did not believe there were still gringos in Caracas, let alone female gringos who fancied his dilapidated SUV. We visited a friendly old man with a fetching '79 Range Rover; he told us he wanted $5000 for it and, in the same breath, kindly explained how we could pop start it: the ignition had not worked in years. I began to lose hope, eyeing *Se vende* signs in the windows of staid and uninspiring Land Cruisers with a resigned interest. And then I met Samuel.

In a city rife with danger and dishonesty, Samuel, the mechanic friend of a friend, should have been one connection too distant for genuine, spontaneous trust. But that's not really how things function in Caracas, or at least it wasn't then. In spite of *la situación*, the Latin American propensity toward friendly, casual connection and openness was alive and well in 2011. By nature,

I am *not* particularly trusting—urban Midwesterners rarely are—but awkwardness horrifies me (even if I spend many of my waking hours evoking it in one way or another), and I couldn't come up with a graceful way to turn down an offer to visit Samuel's garage-cum-homestead-cum-Chavista hideaway in the mountains to check out a Jeep he was trying to unload.

As it turned out, we had different motives. While I went to Samuel's to buy a car, he had invited me up to court a new friend by dangling the bait of a mint 1989 Woody Wagoneer (lamentably, *not* the curvy original that awakened my bi-car-curiosity but the smarter, squarer, manlier version that merged in the early 90s with the less-lovable Cherokee XJ) before me. It wasn't that I was foreign, or especially interesting; Samuel just liked to make friends, and most of all, he liked to talk. A lot. Physically, he was a short, overfed chipmunk with an impressive handlebar mustache; professionally, a retired cargo pilot and aviation engineer turned mechanic; philosophically, an unabashed Chavista who had no trouble reconciling his politics with his comfortable lifestyle. His family had come to Venezuela from Portugal via Panama when he was young. He had shreds of property in assorted and beautiful parts of the country, a lovely second wife named Marlene, and a bank of stories so rich it could fill Venezuela's languishing coffers even today.

On that first visit, Chris and I were treated to four hours of intense discourse and rounds of tea, snacks and liqueurs before the matter of the Jeep even arose. I did get to look it over and learned its storied past (left in Samuel's safekeeping by a wealthy businessman who'd since relocated to the U.S., it accrued fewer than 5000 kilometers in its first 21 years yet had somehow accumulated at least an hour's worth of tales), but so many other project cars hemmed it in that we couldn't extract it for a test drive. Samuel set the price at $10,000. Before you scoff as anyone foreign rightfully should, the dearth of cars for sale and the fact that everyone needs one to exploit

Venezuela's most tangible social benefit, free gas, inflated used car prices to outrageous heights. Despite its negligible Kelley Blue Book value, years of confirming with average Venezuelans proved to me that my car was worth what it cost.

Round two of the purchasing process was more intense, and more exhilarating. Samuel picked me up at home the next day to take the car for a spin. I've been on plenty of "spins" with potential new cars, but never before had one lasted three hours, gone up and down a small mountain, or included a fully narrated tour of the prettiest districts of a capital city. Not only did I get to know my car, I also learned about several governments preceding Chávez's, the French film *Papillon*, patterns of Portuguese and Spanish immigration to the New World over the decades, and the intricacies of keeping one's pilot license current in Venezuela. Although I have not found practical application for much of what Samuel told me on this or the other happy occasions I spent with him (our friendship continued after money changed hands, of course), he expanded both my knowledge of the world and my love for the place I lived.

All those bureaucratic complexities I'd worried about? They dissolved on the following Monday afternoon as Samuel took me on another tour, this time to a registrar and then a ministry. He exchanged cryptic remarks and token bribes with acquaintances who merrily stamped our heap of photocopied and handwritten documents—this, I confirmed the following year when I faced the new bureaucratic challenge of registering a newborn child in Venezuela, is simply how things are done, for better or worse. By that evening, I had become the overjoyed owner of an overpriced but well-loved *rústico* (SUV, colloquially).

As you'd expect, the actual experience of driving in Venezuela is fodder for another long-winded story, so suffice it to say that our four years of road-tripping and local errands in that Jeep produced far more joy than frustration, though plenty of both. We had our share of scares when the engine started clanking toward nightfall in unfamiliar towns, and I picked up one mechanical skill that involved jiggling two particular wires under the hood to make the engine turn over when all else failed. We returned from one weekender crammed into the cab of a tow truck with the Jeep riding ruefully behind. But that car also braved more than a few barrios (usually by accident), forded streams and crossed the *llanos*, and best of all, brought our son Cormac home from the hospital for the first time.

Most people know that right now in 2017, Venezuela is going through a devastating crisis at the hands of an incompetent government. Things will likely get worse before they get better, and the horror and uncertainty that Venezuelans face is the stuff of nightmares. With this in mind, it seems unbefitting to write such a frivolous chronicle of our time there. But reports of *la situación* are being churned out by the dozen each day, penned by people far more knowledgeable and qualified than me. In spite of the tyranny and anguish, life goes on, and my five years in Caracas showed me that Venezuelans are resilient and will continue to find some joy in their lives and each other while weathering this storm. For people like me, who lived there with the luxury of choosing when to leave, it was easy to see beyond (or hide from?) the chaos and despair, and cruising around in that car was the best way I found to don my rose colored glasses and glimpse the magic.

The Jeep, incidentally, was passed onto a colleague for half the price that I had paid. This colleague was young, tattooed, rugged and charming, in the way of a well-preserved Subaru Brat from the 80s. He had even less sense than I do. By the time his name was officially on the title, he had already bribed a policeman and, on a different occasion, destroyed a brand-new pick-up truck when his kayaks (secured by bungee cords) went sailing off the Jeep's roof on the highway. I'm glad the wheels went to someone with a sense of adventure and appreciation of what the country has to offer, though, and hope they're still cruising Venezuela's byways, surviving the potholes and washouts to reach smoother roads ahead.

Jess Barga, a native of Cincinnati, Ohio, teaches in Guangzhou, China. She has taught high school English and Spanish for 15 years, 5 in the US and 10 in South Korea, Venezuela, and China.

MOXIBUSTION
Tian Yuan (Kelly)

Moxibustion cured my grandma's arthritis. Years later, when my mom couldn't lift her right arm up to a horizontal point, moxibustion cured her frozen shoulder; she can now reach her arm across her shoulder and touch her back. I, too, had a problem and the only cure for me was...that's right... moxibustion!** So, you might ask why my family was willing to embrace such a traditional Chinese treatment? Because we are Chinese and I am from the city of Wuxi.

Many years ago, before embarking on my career as an international school teacher, I had a skin problem. I tried many medications and many doctors, but none cured the problem permanently. After observing the success of moxibustion, a treatment involving burning a Chinese herb called ai (pronounced "I") near one's skin to suck out toxins and cold/dampness in the body, I decided to try it myself. Indeed, it cured most of my problems without any side effects. So I brought it with me to Vietnam on my first expat teaching assignment.

While most international teachers are from North America, Europe, Australia, and New Zealand, many of us come from other countries. After starting my teaching career in my hometown of Wuxi, a few years later I decided to move abroad. This was a bold move, one certainly out of character for a single 25-year old Chinese woman. According to social customs, I should already be married and starting a family. Nevertheless, I accepted a position in Ho Chi Minh City.

Back to the moxibustion connection: I knew that the herb used in moxibustion produced a distinct smell. It wasn't until my Slovakian-American friend Daniela visited me that I realized the implications of its peculiar aroma. During one of my treatments, she joked that "'people will think someone's getting high here." Apparently, moxibustion smells like marijuana. Not knowing the smell of the more internationally 'famous' herb, I thought Daniela's observation was funny and left it at that. I didn't think it would be a problem. Until it was.

In Ho Chi Minh City, I lived in a 14-story building where it was common to smell the cooking of our neighbors throughout the hallways. I never realized that my neighbors could also smell the smoke of my moxibustion treatments until I heard a knock on my door. I looked through the peephole. It was the security guard. Opening the door with trepidation, I wondered what he had to say, but I spoke only English and Mandarin and he spoke only Vietnamese. Together, we both spoke "hand gestures." Despite this limitation, I succeeded in convincing him that there was no fire in my apartment and that all was well. Problem solved...or so I thought.

A few days later, another knock. The security guard was back. The next week, several phone calls from someone at the front desk: "Is everything OK?" The next week, another knock. I looked through the peephole yet again, trying to figure out what to say to the security guard. But instead I had to look higher up through the peephole. It wasn't the security guard; it was a Dutch man who lived not one but *two* floors above me. After I explained that what he smelled was an ancient Chinese herb that helps with my skin condition, he smiled and left.

Trying to find a way to not anger my neighbors nor stop my treatments, I sealed the crack between the door and the floor.

But once again, a few days later, another knock on the door. Again I looked higher up in the peephole. The Dutch man was back, banging loudly on the door, arms crossed, brow furrowed.

"I can smell the smoke again!"
Me: "Ok… sorry…"
"Look, I am from Amsterdam, I am a very nice person."
Me: (in my head) "How's that relevant? Why is Amsterdam relevant? Why is being nice relevant?"
"If I smell that again, I'm gonna report you to the building manager."

The smell must have been rising through the ventilators in the kitchen and the bathroom, so I tried to block them both. A couple of days later, it was moxibustion time.

The next day I found myself sitting in the building manager's office.

Complaint after complaint had made it to his desk. I was sure an official ban on my skin treatment was imminent. But much to my surprise, the manager reached down and grabbed something. Seconds later, he laid out the blueprint of my apartment on the table. He pointed to the guest room. "Do it here. Close all the doors."

Here I am. A single Chinese woman in Vietnam.

My neighbors think I'm a drug user.
My apartment manager is helping me continue doing something that other tenants want me to never do again.
A Dutch guy is trying his best to prevent <u>me</u> from doing something that smells like marijuana.

Oh, the oxymorons of moxibustion.

If I ever get another knock on the door, I'll look through the peephole but I may not open it. Because no matter who is waiting on the other side, I know one thing for sure: moxibustion is great.

**For more info on moxibustion, feel free to read this brief article:
<u>*http://tinyurl.com/moxibustioninfo*</u>

Tian Yuan (Kelly), a native of Wuxi, China, teaches in Ho Chi Minh City, Vietnam. She has taught ESL and K-12 Chinese for 7 years, 3 in China and 4 in Vietnam.

THE FOREIGNER CARD
Autum Callender and Sara Stoolman Doerfler

Korea is a place with a plethora of *soju, kimchi*, and amazing public transportation. It is a place where magical friendships are formed and where a particular group of friends took on the status of "family."

Stoolz, the ringleader in this story, found the perfect couch for her new apartment on a Craigslist deep dive. She convinced a few soccer teammates—Rockstar, Autum, and Shorty—to help move the 9 foot couch. But this move wasn't going to happen using the luxury of a car, truck, or moving van…it would all be on foot: above ground walking on the street and below ground taking the subway. After a Sunday game on the military base in Seoul, they hopped on the subway and, in typical Stoolz fashion, mapped out their route as they went instead of researching beforehand. It was twenty-five stations (including four transfers) away. Counting walking, the trip would take almost three hours.

They walked into a mildew-smelling basement apartment where they were greeted by "Captain Craigslist," the seller of the couch. The cushions were shoved into a clear garbage bag; Autum tied them to her back like a backpack and also carried the couch footstool on her head. Shorty and Stoolz worked together to carry the longer portion of the couch while Rockstar grabbed the smaller end piece. Using the Captain's directions, they navigated to the subway for the journey of a lifetime.

As they went down flights of stairs, locals offered to help them carry the furniture onto the train. The soccer players-turned-movers took up the entire end of a subway car. Autum, the social butterfly, sat with her humpback of cushions and offered locals to sit comfortably on the couch, all the while drinking the eggnog she procured en route. The other three stood in the corner laughing at the absurdity of the situation. Each transfer point became a huge challenge as the crew navigated the couch through the masses that ride the Seoul subway every day. Once, a subway conductor actually closed the doors just as they approached the car. With a warm smile, he kindly reopened the doors and allowed the group to enter.

After the weary ladies arrived at the final subway stop, they exited next to a huge Christmas tree, assembled the couch, and took a picture to document what it truly means to carry "The Foreigner Card," the unspoken understanding that foreigners are often excused from doing strange things.

Autum Callender, a military brat, teaches in Atyrau, Kazakhstan. She has taught early childhood, special education, and high school for 13 years, 3 in the US and 10 in Papua New Guinea, China, Korea, Egypt and Kazakhstan.

Sara Stoolman Doerfler, a native of Omaha, Nebraska, teaches in Yangon, Myanmar. She has taught 3rd grade and 6th grade language arts for 11 years, 2 in the US and 9 in South Korea and Myanmar.

A DELICATE SITUATION
Amy Bokser

"We will never have a baby," I keep saying, waiting for someone to prove me wrong.

Instead of a baby, we have a sketchy Mexican adoption lawyer. We're Americans living in Mexico, so our agency in the US connected us with a local lawyer who asked us to meet him at the mall. Now, in a bizarre twist on the famous mall game "That's Your Boyfriend," my husband and I sit together on a bench, muttering about every man who walks past, "That's our lawyer."

"That's our lawyer," I joke about a fat guy wearing sunglasses, black *guayabera* stretched across his hairy chest, and gold chains. He walks over and introduces himself.

He has a deep, almost hypnotic voice. We learn that when he's about to lie to us, to bring up some new issue or say the opposite of what he has previously said, his voice gets deeper. He favors the preface, "As I told you before." As in, "As I told you before, none of my birthmothers are tested for HIV." But that comes later.

The lawyer matches us with birthmother #1. In her photo, she wears glasses and a cross around her neck. We receive a file of "psycho-social information," from which we learn that she has no known diseases and likes "doing things with her hands."

Could we meet her? "Well, as I told you before, that would be a very delicate situation." The agency requires piles of reading for prospective parents about open adoption. Apparently they don't make the lawyer do the same.

Then suddenly he tells us that she's excited to meet us, and we make a date. The day before our meeting, he calls to tell us she has miscarried.

Did he know she had miscarried when we made the date? How do we mourn this loss when we don't know if the mother really existed? I relate these questions to a co-worker. She tells me, helpfully, that it is common for a miscarriage to make you temporarily paranoid.

My students are reading *The Giver*, a futuristic novel in which birthing is a job and newborns are assigned. I don't share my students' horror when they find out about the familial logistics. We wind up having a long discussion about adoption. After class, one of my students waits for me.

"Miss," she says. "I want to tell you something. I'm adopted!"

"That's so cool!" I tell her, glad for her that this is my immediate reaction.

She smiles shyly, and says, "I know." Her evident pride warms my cold ice cube of a heart.

"Can you keep a secret?" I ask her. She nods, all serious. "My husband and I are going to adopt a baby."

"Miss!" she smiles up at me. "THAT'S so cool."

"I know!" I say, and we both laugh. "But you can't tell anyone until it happens."

"I won't," she promises. She's eleven. But I never hear it mentioned again.

My co-worker teaches yoga after school. She's all about positive thinking and creating our own realities. "What about people in concentration camps?" I inquire. She has no response.

The lawyer finds us birthmother #2. She's four months pregnant, twenty years old. Pretty. Her last name, Nieves, means ice cream or snow.

Don't believe the fairy tale.

We meet her over breakfast. She doesn't smile very much, but that can hardly be expected. She agrees with the lawyer that she wants to finish her schooling. She and I order the same thing: hotcakes and a small orange juice. It's a sign! I can't eat any of my hotcakes, but I'm happy to say that she wolfs them down. And she doesn't order coffee. Or sushi.

Nervously, I tell my co-worker about her. I want the telling to make her real, but at the same time, I'm afraid it will make her disappear. My co-worker listens kindly, then invites me to a yoga class for expectant mothers.

Next meeting. The birthmother is noticeably larger. She has forgotten to bring paperwork about medical tests. She doesn't look much happier than she did at our first meeting. Our agency caseworker assured us that the birthmothers receive counseling, but further inquiries reveal that the "counseling" is done by our lawyer.

My husband takes out his camera, asks if he can take a picture. The lawyer is not in it. The birthmother, on the other hand, vogues and preens for the camera. She sticks out her pregnant belly and laughs. Actually, she glows.

But at our next phone conversation with the lawyer, we dare to ask about the medical tests, one of which is a test for HIV. "Does she look sick to you?" he asks. I've begun to wonder if he knows what HIV is, so I start to explain. "It's a delicate situation," he interrupts me, "to ask her for those tests." The tests that are guaranteed on the agency's website? He brushes me off. "She's a little depressed," he says.

The next time I check the website, all mention of those tests has disappeared.

Our next appointment arrives. She tells us about some self-help books she likes, and we write down the author. She tells us the name she's picked out for the baby, but when we ask how to spell it she says it doesn't matter.

She has brought the medical tests. We look through them afterwards in the car. There is no HIV test.
The caseworker is defensive on the phone.

"The birthmothers are screened for HIV," she says.

"Screened?" I reply. "By the lawyer? The way he counsels them too? So if he doesn't think they're HIV positive, they don't get tested?"

"You can ask him for the test," she says. "But I can't force anyone to do anything."

I appeal to the lawyer's better nature when we phone him. I explain that we got HIV tests; we had to get a whole battery of tests to get approved to adopt. We got psychological tests too, both in the US and Mexico. There's so much I can't control in this situation; I want to have peace of mind about one thing, to know that my baby is healthy. "Your baby?" he replies. "This is her baby until she makes the decision." Predictably, I begin to cry. His voice grows deeper. "Do you want me to tell her you do not want her baby if she does not get this test?"

My husband picks up the extension. "Of course we don't want you to say that. But the test is important."

"As I told you before," he begins. So I hang up.

The baby is due this week. The lawyer originally said we could meet them at the hospital, but now, as he told us before, that's not a good idea. He has shown us a blurry sonogram, explaining what we know is not true, that better sonograms just aren't available in Mexico. The HIV question has been put on hold. We've talked to pediatricians about testing once the baby is born. We wait.

The phone rings.

My husband answers it. The worst is not even what he says afterwards; it's the broken sound of his voice. My husband is an optimist. He's the counterpoint to my sarcasm; the base to my acid. And now he's broken. I hug the pieces.

The lawyer says he is sorry. Apparently the birthmother has disappeared. He gives us, for some inexplicable reason, what he says is her cell phone number. We call it, and it rings and rings. We send a text into the ether. Where it stays.

We take a long weekend, vacation at the beach. We sit on a white bench on a boardwalk and cry as we promise each other to enjoy life more from now on. We'll go out to dinner. We'll make more friends. We'll buy a Wii. We'll fly to Barcelona. We're not giving up, but we are going to be happy while we wait for that baby. Happy!

We switch lawyers. It turns out the agency works with another Mexican lawyer. This one is based in Tijuana, half a country away. "She's a little flaky," the caseworker warns.

But the lawyer hooks us up quickly with birthmother #3. She's seven months pregnant and can't afford to keep it; her parents know and are supportive of her decision. The lawyer starts to tell us more. But I zone out. I don't really care what she does in her free time.

Months pass. We don't tell anyone. I smile brightly at school and teach my students about intransitive verbs. We don't get a Wii, but we dive heavily into The Sopranos. The baby is due any day. And yet we've made plans to go to Barcelona next month, because who are we kidding? We will never have a baby.

I'm at school, prepping. My students are starting a new novel, one about magic and Greek gods. But I can't concentrate. The baby's due date was yesterday but we've heard nothing. And I know something is wrong.

I call my husband from my classroom. He has just gotten off the phone with the lawyer. He doesn't sound broken; he sounds flat. Like nothing; like he is no one. "She had the baby," he tells me without preamble. "It was a boy. Her father decided that they would keep it."

We do not have a baby, I realize. We will never have a baby.

I realize that before, I never really thought those words were true.

I scream, I rant, I yell curses. I turn away from the classroom door, where I can see students walking by. "So what the hell are we supposed to do now?" I hurl into the phone. "It's funny you should ask that," says my husband, though he sounds anything but amused. "Because they have this other baby…"

It takes me about ten minutes to do the 25-minute drive home from school.

The other baby is two weeks old. In the photograph they email us, he is very hairy. "He's kind of strange-looking," says my husband. "That's because he's a baby," I say. I will defend him! His eyes are closed. He has a very distinctive forehead; kind of a widow's peak. I think I love him.

Birthmother #4 can fly down tomorrow with him and the lawyer. She has to fly with him because he's legally hers. If they don't do it tomorrow, they won't be available again for two weeks. I say the only thing I can say: I want him.

My husband isn't so sure. "They've jerked us around so much," he says. "Maybe we should think about it. Try our plan of enjoying our lives. Or at least wait the two weeks."
I take a breath.

"I don't want to wait, really sad, for the next baby. I don't want to spend any more months crying. We need him. We need this baby. And he…" but I can't speak anymore. Apparently my vocal cords are tied to my sarcasm cords. And there's no more sarcasm left inside me.

We wait at the airport the next day. Despite our nervous jokes to the contrary, they walk towards us. The birthmother smiles awkwardly, hands us a tiny bundle. Her face crumples for a moment as she tells him good-bye. The lawyer is matter-of-fact. And then we are alone with the most perfect small person the world has ever seen.

His eyebrows. Like little silk square root signs. His lashes are about 64 feet long. He looks serious, like a tiny head of state. A blister in the middle of one small red lip. He sleeps and sleeps. We have a baby.

I won't make you hear about the next three years of paperwork and court meetings before our adoption is finalized. I won't even tell you about the police raid on the first lawyer's office, or his escape and the fact that he's still at large. And I won't tell you much about Charlie, who is mad with excitement about his sixth birthday this month. He loves ninjas, fast shoes, making art, and will eat broccoli only if a speed competition is involved.

I'll just tell you one more thing about my student, who still likes to stop by my desk to look at photos and chat about my son. "You love him SO MUCH," she said one day, dreamily. "He's like your gift from God." And the sarcastic person inside me tried to disagree. But I couldn't.

Amy Bokser, a native of Queens, New York, teaches in Guadalajara, Mexico. She has taught middle school language arts for 18 years, 5 in the US and 13 in Mexico.

HOMINID IN A BOX
George Robinson

It's another gorgeous day in the "Land of the Queen of Sheba." The air is crisp and the lingering hint of eucalyptus smoke hangs in the air. The laughter and thumping of elementary school feet punctuate the scraps of conversation at the annual school carnival. It is October 26, 1974. "Hi, Mr. and Mrs. Robinson. Having a good time?"

"Hi, Peggy. Yes, this is really a fun school carnival. You seniors seem to have this event down pat."

"Thanks. We love organizing this event. Everyone just pitches in and has a good time. Do you remember when I told you that I spent the summer at an archeological dig in the Rift Valley?"

"Sure. As I recall I told you that we have always been into archaeology and particularly into the study of early man and the search for his origin. Dr. Louis Leaky's discoveries at the Olduvai Gorge on the eastern Serengeti Plains in Tanzania are of particular interest. His find predated all other finds in the world and shifted opinion on the rise of man from Central Asia to East Africa. His son Richard is now continuing his work."

Peggy then proceeds to invite us for dinner along with two scientists with whom she worked with on the dig. Both the American paleontologist Don Johanson and the French geologist and paleoanthropologist Maurice Taieb will join for dinner. They are in Ethiopia to review a new find of hominid remains that are nearly 3 million years old. The find consists of half of an upper jaw and half of a lower jaw of a manlike creature and a complete upper jaw and palate of another of the same species. Now, we are really looking forward to this get together.

After arriving and making introductions, we let the archeologists know that we have been keenly following their recent discovery. Don and Maurice explain that the complete upper has all of its teeth intact now. Originally two were missing but they were found and put into place. This is one of the most important finds in the last 20 years. Now, all the textbooks must be rewritten. At that point, Don casually pulls out a Dutch Master cigar box from a backpack close by, opens it, and carefully unwraps the cotton it contained. We move the coffee table, set our drinks aside and sink down on the pristine white sheepskin rug, watching as Don gently lays the specimens out one by one. First, one of an apelike creature, including the upper jaw fragment, then the lower jaw half of the hominid. "The preservation and completeness of this is remarkable!"

Don smiles and said, "It gets better." Then he pulls out the upper half and the complete upper.

Shocked disbelief escapes our mouths with an audible gasp! Here we are, sitting on the living room floor, and displayed on the white sheepskin rug before us is one of the greatest finds in history! We examine the specimens closely as the three scientists and the high school senior smile like doting parents at our amazed wonder.

"I wonder what Richard will say?"
"He'll say that we just provided further proof of his theory."

They are referring, of course, to Richard Leaky, who will respond in exactly that fashion in subsequent news articles and interviews.

And that is how we got introduced to Lucy's sister, lovingly cradled in a Dutch Master cigar box! A few weeks later, Johanson and Taieb found Lucy, to this day one of the most important finds of hominid fossils, tracing the origins of man.

These are just the kind of people I had hoped we would meet when we came here!

Dr. George Robinson, a native of Topeka, Kansas, retired in 2014. He taught math, physics, and was an administrator at all levels, as well as director of schools for 40 years, 7 in the US and 33 in Ethiopia, the Kingdom of Saudi Arabia, Malaysia, Morocco, the United Arab Emirates, and South Africa.

THE HOUSE OF SHARING
Jennifer Ribachonek

Our stories only exist inside our heads
Inside our ravaged bodies
Inside a time and space of war
And emptiness
There is no paper trail
Nothing official on the books
Only conscience
Only this.
   Eve Ensler, "Say It" (For the Comfort Women)

The bus takes us southeast out of the sea of high rises of suburban Seoul into the rolling hills and rural beauty of Gwangju. We are seven teachers on a field trip of sorts—all women, all foreigners in South Korea—and our destination on this Sunday morning is the House of Sharing. The House of Sharing is the sum of its parts: a non-profit organization, a nursing home, a cemetery, a museum, a temple, a sculpture garden, a place of protest, a place of healing. It is the only place like it in the world, and the seven women who live here have a story to share with arms and doors wide open to all who come and listen. We went. We listened.

I first learned about the experience of the Korean "Comfort Women" through the words of Eve Ensler's work of activist theater, *The Vagina Monologues*. Ensler's play sheds light on a host of women's issues, using a diverse gathering of female stories and voices. The expression "Comfort Women" is misleading and inadequate; young Korean girls were abducted by the Japanese army, systematically forced into sex slavery, scattered to Japanese "comfort" stations all over Asia, and repeatedly raped. Not for days and weeks, but for months and years. Today, these survivors of military sexual slavery by the Japanese Army are respectfully referred to in Korea as Halmoni, or "Grandmothers." Their stories are brutal. Woman after woman endured a tragedy so profound it is hard to imagine. But their time spent as sex slaves was just the beginning, for the Halmoni's experiences were then compounded by over 40 years of collective silence, shame, stigmatization, and shunning after the war.

When we step off the bus, we receive a warm welcome by the English-speaking, college-aged volunteers who work with the Halmoni. We watch a documentary about the experience of Kim Hak-Soon, the Halmoni who broke the 48-year silence when she became the first-ever survivor to speak up publicly in Korea about being a sex slave for the Japanese army during WWII. Her courage inspires the next generation of Koreans and these four young volunteers to seek justice for the Halmoni.

The volunteers lead us into the living room of the group home, where five of the Grandmothers are sitting. I join a few other people to sit and talk with Kim Kung-Ja, one of the oldest women living in the house, born in 1926. She is wearing pink pants, a yellow shirt, a colorful scarf, and a serious look. One of the volunteers translates for us. Halmoni Kim sits in a chair with her legs folded, a position that was comfortable for her very swollen ankle; she can no longer sit cross-legged on the floor. Through the interpreter, we make polite conversation and learn that her favorite season is winter because she does not like to sweat. I sit mostly silent. She tells us how she used to be a devout Buddhist but later became a devout Catholic who rises for prayer at 4 a.m. Through her faith, she searches for the truth about her life. According to Halmoni Kim, it was this search for meaning that helped her survive all she had to endure in this life of isolation and shame. She has no family and very few friends. While not frail, she suffers from multiple health issues related to her internal organs. All the women in the House of Sharing have complications and ailments of their ruined reproductive and urological systems. Despite these serious problems, life at the House of Sharing is comfortable and healing in its structures and schedules. The Grandmothers repeatedly receive visitors and share their humanity with grace.

Halmoni Kim is quiet as she carefully watches the clock, anticipating the lunch that will be promptly served at noon. We learn from the interpreter that Halmoni is punctual and lateness is a cause of stress for her. The visiting time is over. We pose for a picture, help her walk to the dining area, and say goodbye.

Unlike any nursing home that I have ever visited, the complex includes a Museum of Sexual Slavery, just steps from where the Grandmothers live. The volunteers lead us inside to the main floor, which contains important historical information, photographs, and documents. But the real tour, the part that sticks with me even to this day, starts after beginning to descend the long spiral ramp into the basement. At first a larger-than-life map shows the hundreds of "comfort stations" that were scattered all over China, Japan, Korea, and SE Asia.

When the war ended and the "comfort stations" closed, the women who had not died were just left on their own…left in whatever remote Indonesian or Philippine island or Chinese village they were brought to. Official Japanese documents on display state that the purpose of "comfort stations" was to prevent rape crimes of local women in the invaded countries. Other documentation shows the inhumane treatment of the women—the venereal diseases, the torture used, the number of soldiers the women were required to serve. The number of women forced into sexual slavery by the Japanese is estimated to be between 50,000 and 200,000. The information is heartbreaking.

The spiraling ramp into darkness continues. At the bottom, we see a life-size replica of a so-called "comfort station" cubicle. On the door hangs rows of wooden blocks on hooks, each block with a flower name representing a sex slave. When a woman was unavailable for the Japanese army due to venereal disease or pregnancy, her block was turned over. In Japan, many restaurants use this same method of displaying the menu of available items to order. Taking turns, we step inside the tiny wooden cubicle, which has a bed, a washbowl, a lamp and a small window. It is simple and horrifying. It is difficult to breathe. The bed has a blanket. Under the blanket are many small pieces of paper with writing obscured by a single fold. The volunteer explains that these are sorrowful notes left by students who visit the Museum. Many of those are from Japanese students.

Not coincidentally, when we begin our ascent back toward the top, the tone changes. Sunlight pours into a room where we see portraits of surviving Halmoni. Next to the portraits are pictures and documents of the weekly Wednesday protest in front of the Japanese embassy in Seoul. This effort, begun in 1992, is credited as being the world's longest lasting protest. What the Halmoni want, before they die, is to hear the Japanese government acknowledge and apologize to the former "Comfort Women" for what was done to them. There is an alcove, lit with candles, displaying gifts from Museum visitors—works of art, posters of solidarity, and thousands upon thousands of folded paper cranes from tourists and school children, once again, many of whom are Japanese. Seeing the sheer quantity of that simple symbol of peace and reconciliation moves me to tears.

The museum ends with an art gallery that displays pictures and paintings created by the Halmoni who were offered music and art therapy as a service to process their trauma. The paintings depict graphic scenes of brutality and torture but also offer glimpses of the occasional peace that these women in their dying years have experienced. The theme of justice prevails in their artwork and in this exhibition area.

It is this healing power of art that gives me pause and moves me to reflect on my life's journey so far. I recognize the privilege I have growing up in a loving home, nurturing an activist's yearn for social justice, working as an international teacher, and raising a family with a loving, patient partner. I believe in the promise of community and the magic that happens when a group of people with a shared vision for raising humanity supports each other. I give thanks for artists and storytellers and the creativity that lives in each of us even in the face of unspeakable horror. In my cluttered mind I whisper a vow to keep learning, listening, loving and living wherever I find myself.

Before leaving the museum, we all take a few moments to reflect. The volunteers know the emotional space we are now in—so different from when we arrived—and respond accordingly. As we walk toward the bus to leave, we meet Halmoni Kim Soon-Ok, who is returning from the church where she spends her Sundays. She smiles broadly, giving each of us a tight strong hug. She is sorry she missed us and tells us we are welcome to come back and visit anytime. I have not been physically back to The House of Sharing after that moment, but I have been back there in spirit a thousand times since.

Jennifer Ribachonek, a native of Hollywood, Florida, lives in Istanbul, Turkey. She has taught EAL and learning support for 14 years in Mexico, Costa Rica, South Korea, and Turkey.

HUMBLED IN UZBEKISTAN
Joyce van den Hoven

Tashkent, Uzbekistan—I'd never even heard of the city, let alone the country, when I went to the London job fair five years ago. To this day, my friends still refer to it as "Where-is-it-stan." I had initially hoped to get a job somewhere in Europe, but throughout the recruiting weekend I decided that I should 'go with the curveball' and accept an offer in Tashkent. I don't regret it for a second.

Tashkent is best described as a quirky, slightly weird but amazing place. During my first year "only in Uzbekistan" became a regular saying. But, after a while, the quirkiness became normal to me.

One of the biggest differences I initially encountered was food shopping. In Scotland, the big 24-hour supermarket down the road had everything from cornflakes to cupcake cases. In Tashkent, a 'big' supermarket is the size of an average one in the UK, and while the essentials were all available, everything I wanted was not.

As a keen baker and cake decorator, I was presented with quite a few challenges to source ingredients. For instance, at first I was told one can only buy icing sugar from the American Embassy Commissary. This isn't actually the case, and I quickly learned I needed to keep asking around. Locals will usually know where to find what you are looking for. Indeed, Uzbeks are some of the friendliest and helpful people I have ever met.

It didn't take long before I was introduced to the local foods, including the fantastic Uzbek bread 'non' ('lepyoshka' in Russian), a type of leavened flatbread typical of many Central Asian countries. Each local region has its own twist on the recipe and design, but all the ones I had seen are round with a flat circle in the middle created by a bread stamp. I saw them being made and baked in the tandir ovens at the market, but, as a baker, I really wanted to give it a go myself.

I started asking the local staff at my school if they had any connections. One colleague put me in touch with the local bread seller in his neighbourhood, and we set the date for one evening when I could meet with two bakers. As I was interested in learning the entire process from start to finish (including making the dough), I was invited to come back at 6 a.m. to make the second batch. However, finding my way back to the bakery the following morning proved to be a bit of a challenge. Many of the streets in residential neighbourhoods look the same to me, and street names (if there are any to start with) aren't really any use. However, by following my nose, I found the bakery; after all, who can mistake the smell of freshly baked bread?

To say the workspace was tiny would be an understatement. The room was roughly 3x3 meters with a small domestic stove, a sink, a trough the size of a large crib for the dough, one long table and two shorter ones. Judging by the *korpachas* (thin mattresses stuffed with cotton) I saw tucked neatly under the tables, this space must also double as their sleeping quarters. The *tandir* oven was in an adjoining space.

I didn't speak any Uzbek aside from "please" and "thank you," and my Russian only reached as far as trips to the market and taxi rides home. Neither of the bakers spoke any English, so communication was mainly through hand gestures which sufficed quite well for making bread.

In my broken Russian, I was able to respond to questions regarding where I was from, how old I was, and, of course, the ever popular question, whether I was married. In Uzbekistan, women tend to get married in their early twenties. Since I am in my late thirties and usually want to avoid further queries, I typically answer yes. However, I didn't feel comfortable lying to these two bakers who had opened up their home and business to me, so I told them the truth, "no, I'm not married."

This information was immediately communicated to the two ladies responsible for selling the bread. The question was asked again and again, and their stern looks gave me the impression they felt I really should be married by now and have some children. Around midday, one of the ladies asked me *why* I wasn't married. I did my best to tell her I felt I didn't need a husband; I was happy without one. Her whole demeanour changed instantly. With a big smile on her face, a couple of waving hand gestures and a whole string of incomprehensible Russian, I understood she agreed with me. She seemed to indicate that husbands were good for nothing anyway; I was better off without one!

A few hours after my arrival, I was surprised when one of the bakers called a friend who did speak English and put him on speaker phone. A 10-minute three-way conversation ensued with the friend doing his best to translate for the bakers. They had many questions that had clearly been on their minds since I got there. They wanted to know if I had siblings, where my family lived, and what I was doing in Tashkent. Some might see these questions as being nosy, but people here are just really interested in learning about you and life outside their country. Very few have the opportunity or resources to travel abroad so they try to learn as much as they can, when they can.

Word had obviously spread that there was a foreigner present, as many people began lingering around and looking in. This included an official-looking gentleman who, I quickly learned, was the chief of the *mahalla* (neighbourhood). I was promptly whisked away to visit the town hall and asked to pose for pictures with him and another official-looking lady who was apparently in charge of all the women living in the *mahalla*. A teenage girl, with a good level of English, was found to translate.

I genuinely thought I was only going to be at the bakery for a couple of hours. Fortunately, I hadn't planned anything else as I finally left around 5 p.m. when the last *lepyoshkas* came out of the oven. I was allowed to participate in the entire process— from making and kneading the dough, shaping it into the balls for the first proof, and then further shaping, cutting and stamping them into the correct shape for baking. They even allowed me to place the bread on the inside wall of the oven and take it out with the basket-type scraper.

Every time I thought it was time for me to go, something else happened to prevent my departure. Whether it was the English phone call, the *mahalla* visit, or the tasty food they made for me, I wanted to make sure I didn't act rude and offend anyone by leaving at the wrong time.

The two bakers and the female bread sellers were generous and friendly, truly epitomizing traditional Uzbek hospitality in every sense of the word. I was, and still am, incredibly honoured and humbled they allowed me to join them. This day is still, by far, the absolute highlight of my time in Uzbekistan.

While it is comforting to remain in familiar settings, with a familiar language and foods, I encourage everybody to step out of their comfort zone. There may be some hiccups and difficulties along the way, but teaching overseas gives you opportunities to collect life-changing and unforgettable experiences you otherwise would never have.

Joyce van den Hoven was born in Antwerp, Belgium but lived in the UK for about half her life. She has been a secondary Learning/ Student Support teacher for 15 years, 9 in Belgium and the UK and 6 in the US and Uzbekistan.

MAY YOU LIVE IN
INTERESTING TIMES
Kathryn Williams Smith

To live in interesting times may be the end result of a Chinese curse, but it is the fascinating nature of the world today that drives many of us to become international teachers in the first place. It is not enough to simply *visit* other parts of the world—we want to *live* there and become immersed in the culture, language, food and unique experiences that are the essence of living abroad. We are inherently risk-takers. Despite this inclination, we also do not want to be featured in the lead story on CNN. We want to live in "interesting times," but not too interesting.

What happened to me in 2011 both confirmed and challenged this idea.

Back in 1999, I took a huge risk: I jettisoned my career as an environmental lawyer to become a middle school teacher. Before the mid-career shift to a much lower paying job, my family had planted roots in the Washington, D.C. area. There, I fully expected to stay safe and snug for quite a long time, perhaps even my entire adult life. But when my husband's management consulting firm offered him a position to expand a branch office in Mexico City just one year later, we jumped at the chance to take our family abroad. We enrolled our children in an international school where I was quickly scooped up as a foreign teacher employed as a "local hire," a huge benefit for the school because, in addition to paying me only a fraction of a regular teacher's salary, it did not have to provide housing, shipping, medical insurance, and more. But I did not care about the salary differential—I was doing what I loved (teaching) in a country with so many rich cultural experiences for my entire family. It really was a win-win for both the school and the Smiths.

After Mexico, the pattern repeated itself in Peru and Costa Rica: husband finds job, family moves, children enroll in international schools, and I teach as a "local hire."

Perhaps we were lulled into a false sense of security by spending those ten years in Mexico, Peru, and Costa Rica without any incident greater than a stolen car or minor earthquake tremors. Or perhaps it was the timing of making a decision after a third round of happy hour mojitos on a beach in Costa Rica. Either way, in 2010, we threw caution to the wind and agreed that it was a great idea for my husband to take a position with USAID in Afghanistan. Unlike previous jobs where our entire family tagged along, Afghanistan was an "unaccompanied" post. Knowing the risks my husband would be exposed to in a Taliban-controlled province, we needed to be sure that at least one parent would stay out of harm's way. We also knew that I needed to be closer than Costa Rica if I ever wanted to see my husband during his limited leave trips. (For some reason Kabul to San José is not the easiest of routes.) In addition, our children had already graduated from high school and were attending universities in Tokyo and

Edinburgh. The best choice at the time to see my husband and children turned out to be teaching at the Schutz American School in Alexandria, Egypt, a large port city known for its role as a leader in the ancient world and as a less chaotic city when compared to nearby Cairo. While my husband was in dangerous Afghanistan, I could live cocooned on the school campus in a faculty apartment with meals, laundry service and drivers provided for me. The country I lived in had the same leader, Hosni Mubarak, in power for 30 years. I had the safe alternative.

At Schutz, in addition to my teaching duties, I was the faculty advisor for the Model United Nations (MUN) program. For those unfamiliar with MUN, it is extremely impressive. For multiple days, teenage students voluntarily wear business attire, speak in formal language, pretend to be representatives of countries around the world, research, write and debate resolutions to solve the world's most pressing problems, and more. Did I mention they <u>voluntarily</u> do this?! In January 2011, I took a group of students from Alexandria to perhaps the world's largest MUN conference in The Hague where 4,000 students from five continents participate.

Upon arrival in The Hague, my biggest concerns were trying to keep ten high school students out of bars that served alcohol to 16 year olds and watching for suspicious baked goods that are available in Amsterdam. Those quickly became the least of my worries when, on the second day of the week-long conference, thousands of anti-government activists back in Cairo flocked to Tahrir Square in response to a grass-roots, social media-driven protest against the Egyptian government. Three days later, when we were scheduled to fly back home, the Arab Spring had sprung, and Egypt was in the middle of a firestorm as the streets of both Cairo and Alexandria erupted in riots over the recalcitrant Hosnai Mubarak and his government's failure to resolve the problems of Egypt.

No one had predicted that this revolution would occur after three decades of the same leadership. Heck, I was still in college when Mubarak came into power in 1981 after Egyptian president Anwar Sadat was assassinated. Despite the myriad reasons for reformers demanding change—Mubarak's ability to maintain power through stronger police power, legalized censorship, the suspension of constitutional rights, corruption, and surviving six (6!) assassination attempts as well as problems of rising food prices and youth unemployment—it was still quite surprising that it was actually happening. And it was happening in the country I now lived…but I wasn't there. I was in the Hague. With 10 students.

Personally, I wouldn't have minded staying in the comfort of one of the safest cities in Europe, but I was also feeling the strain of being the only adult responsible for the welfare of ten over-stimulated teenagers. After consulting our school administrators, parents, and Egypt Air, everyone was confident that we could return to Alexandria via Cairo without incident. By the time we arrived in Cairo, contrary to earlier assurances, Egypt Air announced that our flight to Alexandria had been cancelled. On top of that, there was no indication of when, or even if, it would be rescheduled. The eleven of us were stuck in the transit hallway of Egypt Air with no access to food, water or public toilets; even Tom Hanks in *The Terminal* had access to those amenities. At this point the times were becoming a little 'too' interesting.

But it was at this moment that I discovered just how resourceful, resilient, and, thankfully, well-connected my students were. Every one of them immediately got on their cell phone to call someone—parents, grandparents, their cousin's husband's father's friend—all in an effort to get us out of the airport and home to Alexandria. They not only convinced the perplexed airline staff to bring us the food that would have been served to us on our flight, but, more importantly, they reached someone high enough in the Egypt Air hierarchy who scheduled a flight just for us. While we waited, my unperturbed students played music on their phones, used their iPads, or slept on the floor without a care in the world!

When our plane finally arrived in Alexandria, the small but usually crowded airport was eerily empty, and a large army tank was sitting ominously at the end of the airport driveway. Apparently, as the protesters took to the streets, looters, who always seem to crawl out of societies' dark corners in trying times, were creating havoc in cities across Egypt. These looters and the potential for armed conflict had me the most disconcerted. Since few, if any, trusted the police (too corrupt, too brutal), groups of Egyptian men were out on the streets with bats, clubs, and kitchen knives as a sort of vigilante neighborhood watch to make sure no one looted their businesses or broke into their homes. At one point, there was a major altercation in front of our campus gate. Warning gunshots were fired to stave off potential looters. Members of our staff and I scrambled around looking for bottles, baseball bats, and golf clubs—anything we could use as weapons. As it turned out, we were relatively safe because our neighbors, as part of their neighborhood watch, were protecting the school. Still, when the offer came a few days later for the foreign teachers to take a charter plane out of Egypt, most of us decided that it would be better to be in the US saying "we didn't need to leave" than to be sitting in Alexandria saying "we should have gone."

The two weeks that I spent back in the US are best summed up as surreal. Perhaps it was jet lag, but far more likely it was the juxtaposition of leaving a world in chaos to arriving in a world of order. I think it struck me most one evening when I was walking on a DC street and realized that it was deathly quiet. No honking horns, no prayers from a minaret, no people yelling, no dogs barking or cats yowling, no babies crying, no vendors seeking used goods, no trams rattling or train whistles blowing or any of the constant background noise that is Egypt.

In fact, there was virtually no noise at all except the heels of my boots on the concrete sidewalk. And why would there be? It was 10 p.m. on a weeknight; most people were at home settling down for the night.

Oddly, I felt more uneasy walking on that silent street than I had in the cacophony of Alexandria. Maybe that's how Dorothy felt when she returned to Kansas—glad to be home, but a little disoriented.

As things started to calm down in Egypt, we all returned to our Alexandria classrooms. Initially there were few, if any, police working in the city. At that time there were a number of reported muggings, home invasions, gang related assaults and murders. I'm not sure how many of these actually happened...the Egyptian people love a good story—the more fantastic, the better. I heard enough rumors and conspiracy theories in the months that followed to keep Oliver Stone busy for a lifetime, so it was difficult to sort out what the risk factor really ended up being. Whatever it was, it was likely far less than the perception.

While my husband knew he was moving to a place that potentially was "too" interesting, I had no idea my "safe" choice of Alexandria was going to experience tremendous upheaval 6 months after arrival. There are many reasons I never want to be that close to a revolution again, but living through a momentous time in history is also rather exhilarating. In contrast to the calm of The Hague and D.C, living in Alexandria in early 2011 made me realize that sometimes it is OK to be "cursed" enough to live and teach in incredibly interesting times.

Kathryn Williams Smith, a native of Homer, New York, teaches in Tblisi, Georgia. She has taught high school history for 13 years, 2 in the US and 11 in Mexico, Peru, Costa Rica, Egypt, and Georgia.

ONE NIGHT/BABY IN BANGKOK
Sabrina Mooroogen

I had been living outside of England for three years before I became pregnant with my first child. The choice to have our child born in a place outside of our known sphere, away from our family, was not one that we made lightly. However, having a child abroad was not the strange and scary experience I expected. At least that what I was told.

My co-workers at the St Andrews International School in Rayong, Thailand (near Pattaya) were very supportive, especially those who had already experienced it. There were so many who had become pregnant that, upon arriving in Thailand, the head teacher had quipped that if I wanted a baby, "there was something in the water here in Pattaya!" I drank a lot of that water, got pregnant, and started planning to have my baby in Thailand.

But where to have it? The nearest hospital was in Pattaya, less than a 30 minute drive from our school. It's a beach town far more famous for its 'flavourful' red light district than for any medical facility. It is like no other place I have been to before: it's both fun and energetic, but also deeply sordid and base. In Pattaya, there is a thin line between feeling outraged at society and slowly becoming immune to it.

My husband and I decided that we would prefer the renowned Bumrungrad Hospital in Bangkok. The Pattaya hospital was known for a very high percentage of cesarean sections, while the Bangkok one was known for its quality service—people fly from all over Southeast Asia just to go there. Sounds like a simple choice, but there was one key problem: the Bangkok hospital was TWO hours away. Many colleagues assured me that I would have plenty of time to get there. When I tell people this now, in my adopted hometown of Austin, Texas, they are astounded that I would choose a hospital that far away. But oddities like these are commonplace when living internationally, and what seems like a bad idea in one place (e.g. the US) is perfectly acceptable in another (e.g. Thailand). We made the 4-hour round trip to our doctor appointments and were very happy with the care Bumrungrad provided. Tests were common and thorough, questions were all answered, and the Lamaze classes were well-organized.

It's difficult preparing for a baby, especially the first. It is hard to know what you might need. Two-and-a-half weeks prior to the due date, I was still trying to determine exactly what we should have on hand. My mum was set to fly from England to Thailand near the due date—she was going to bring most of the baby clothes, bedding, and tiny socks. As the nesting instinct settled in, I was sure we needed a humidifier to battle against the harsh air spewed out from the old AC units. (Our unit actually had a nest of bees living in it…that's a whole other story.) My husband and I had set out for the malls of Pattaya in search of this essential item when I started to get that tightening feeling across my stomach. But like almost all first timers, I ignored this sign.

I kept telling myself this: I still have two-and-a-half weeks left.

We made our way to Subway for some meatball subs, and then walked (to be more precise, I waddled) past rows and rows of terrible tourist knick-knacks, uninspiring clothing, sofas, handmade jewelry, a massive grocery store, and hundreds of copied DVDs before giving up. A Thai mall is so massive it seems like it has everything you could ever need, but it doesn't have anything you actually want. Feet sore and tummy tight, we headed back to our unnecessarily massive truck. It was so high off the ground that I had to get on a stepstool and have my husband haul me inside. A fun experience most times, but not when you are over 37 weeks pregnant.

Two hours later, I was lying on my sofa counting the minutes between contractions. From the truck ride to the time in our house, the contractions were getting closer together. But Bangkok is a long ways away and I wasn't due for at least a fortnight. Just in case, I asked for advice. My in-laws are pretty wise...of course I should start with them. Over Skype, they said it was time to leave for the hospital. Just in case, I checked with my parents. They told me the same thing. Even though both of our mothers had given birth to my husband and me, I still needed to ask for some more advice. I messaged my best friend. Her response was simple and effective. "GET TO THE HOSPITAL." 3 for 3. At least they were consistent. But...what did my Lamaze teacher think?! I hadn't asked her yet. The words "I'm sure it is time" sealed the deal. After two sets of parents, my best friend, and the Lamaze teacher, I finally called my doctor. You can guess what he said.

After one more round on the stepstool and into the truck, we were on our way: a 2-hour journey starting at 2:00 a.m. Correction: The trip SHOULD have been just two hours. We made a wrong turn. After joking many times of giving birth in a pineapple field, I realized that maybe we had engaged in foreshadowing instead of simply being funny.

Despite the wrong turn, we made it to the hospital in plenty of time. I started my labor in a private room. To the side was a huge exercise ball—for what I do not know. After awhile, the doctor came in and checked on me. Things were not going fast enough for him. It was OK with us…if by OK you mean husband passed out and wife screaming—I just wanted the epidural! That's when I found out that the hospital, the great hospital that people from other countries fly to just to have their babies, is out of drugs until Monday. They were being sued for an epidural-related death. I wasn't worried about that death…I just wanted the indescribable pain to go back to "describable."

The doctor managed to answer his cell phone and check my dilation at the same time…a true skill. After hanging up, his next words were not pleasing to the ears: "Emergency C-section." Exactly what we were hoping to avoid! One of the reasons we didn't go to the nearby hospital in Pattaya was because C-sections were standard practice there. But here, in Bangkok, what choice did we have? We signed consent forms and were rushed into another room.

I think it was at this point (forgive me if my memory of these few hours aren't crystal clear) that the realization of being very far away, without our families, and barely understanding what was being said around us, started to take its toll. All I could hear were people shouting in Thai. It was disorientating. I felt like something was happening TO me rather than me being the one doing the action.

A little while later, my husband made the mistake of looking to see what was happening, and so out came the smelling salts again. But there she was. My daughter was born! They put her in my arms briefly before taking her away. Again the language barrier baffled us...why was a tube being pushed down her throat? Again no answers. It turned out she had swallowed blood in the process.

Hours later, the three of us were together in a private room at the hospital. We were fine. In fact, we were beyond fine. My husband was no longer passing out and my daughter and I were both feeling good. Our room had its own kitchenette and restaurant service. The amenities were even better than some hotels I had stayed in, so we ended up paying for an extra night! When all was said and done, we had a beautiful, healthy girl who spent the first five months of her life soaking up the Thai sunshine and playing in the sand.

My daughter is now almost five years old, and she loves to hear the drama of her birth. When anyone asks her where she, this daughter of a Mauritian-English woman and a Sicilian-American man who met in Egypt, was born, she proudly tells him or her: "I was born in Thailand—Sawatdee ka!"

Sabrina Mooroogen, a native of Brighton, England, lives in Austin, TX. She taught year 6 (grade 5) for 1 year in England and 5 in Egypt, Qatar and Thailand.

IV. TEACHING OVERSEAS

PROMISES
Cailin Minor

"But I promised myself I would dance." I looked down at the thin, five-year-old Thai boy staring up at me with determined and innocent eyes. "What?" I asked in confusion. "I promised myself I would dance!" He said again with relentless enthusiasm. He was once again talking about dancing at our weekly all-school assembly. "Not this week Channarong," I sighed.

Channarong was an enthusiastic and passionate Thai boy who wowed me on the first day of school by walking into the classroom, ripping off his uniform hulk-style, and then throwing his feet on a chair shouting, "Look what I can do!" I stared open-mouthed while his skinny arms vigorously pumped up and down doing push-ups. Channarong was memorable from day one.

In the 2nd week of the school year, I told my new Kindergarten class that this week we would have our first all-school assembly. A typical assembly involved a message from the principal, singing, and some sharing from different classrooms. The assemblies were planned a week or two in advance and classes could sign up to share what they had been learning. Everything was planned out, leaving little room for improv or last minute artistic requests from five-year-olds.

After my assembly announcement, Channarong approached me and said in a confident voice, "I would like to dance at the assembly." I looked at him in that amused way we reserve for small children and old people when they request ridiculous things. It wasn't clear what the specifics of his "dance performance" would entail, but one could only imagine what a five-year-old would come up with. I politely explained that the assembly was already planned for tomorrow but maybe he could dance at a future assembly. I congratulated myself on handling the awkward situation because "The future" is a magical place where early childhood teachers put all the things they don't want to deal with. Think of it as the Narnia of broken promises and forgotten ambitions.

My victory was short-lived. Much to my dismay, Channarong was right in front of me one week later asking the same question. This time I tried a more direct approach. "No, honey," I said empathetically, "the assemblies are for classes to show what they have been learning, not for individual students to dance or sing."

It seemed like we had cleared up this misunderstanding and could move on, but Channarong would not give up that easily. "But I PROMISED myself I would dance," he said emphasizing the word as if this was all the convincing I would need. I looked down at Channarong with a mixture of annoyance and admiration. I couldn't help but let a laugh escape my lips. Promised himself?! What a dramatic statement, especially from someone so young.

Then I started to wonder, what had I "promised" myself I would do that week? Only drink one glass of wine per week... okay fine, per night? Not spend every minute binge watching Friday Night Lights? Get to the gym and work out for more than 15 minutes? I had a creeping suspicion that this kid not only had more ambition than I did, but also a worthier cause that involved more than half-hearted attempts at healthy living. I quickly brushed aside my momentary self-reflection and stayed the course. "Not this week, Channarong," I sighed.

As the weeks went on Channarong never forgot nor relented, and his catch phrase stuck with me. It was pretty humbling to see this kid feel confident about what he wanted and be willing to put himself out there to achieve it. Reflecting about this years later, I like to think that now and then I can find something that matters that much to me; something that I'll promise myself I'll do, and then take the risk to follow through.

Eventually, Channarong did convince me that he was meant to dance. We found out that the upper school students were holding break dance lessons during the lunch hour and they let us come. Week after week, Channarong practiced and learned to break dance much to the surprise of the older kids. They were so taken with him that they asked this kindergartner to dance in the upper school play. Our elementary principal followed suit and asked Channarong to do a reprisal of his dancing at our weekly all-school assembly.

As the assembly began, I caught his eye and smiled. I could tell he was a little nervous as he scanned the crowd. He gave me a confident grin showing that he knew he'd end up here all along, even if I didn't know it at the time. The music started and loud cheers erupted as Channarong began dancing for the whole school to see...just as he promised himself.

Cailin Minor teaches in Colombia. You may remember her from such stories as "The New Normal."

GROWING MORE INTO WHO I AM
Sarah Marslender

The college essay feels intimidating from the start. Admissions committees judge your merit on GPA, letters of recommendation, and the essay you hope shouts "Like me!" "Choose me!" When I introduce the essay in September, students stress about which prompt might show them best. The first week of drafting is like watching a group of friends pose for pictures, turning a head first this way and then that, popping a hip, kissing the camera, brushing hair from the face, trading a smile for a smirk. They don't know what they want to say about who they are. They don't totally know who they are.

Last year I felt much the same. My seniors were choosing a future they couldn't see. During their college essay drafting and revision work, conversations echoed from one student to the next. Tareq wanted to be a doctor, maybe, or an engineer. Nadine was interested in business. No one wanted to be a literature teacher. I thought how I got here. One afternoon I drafted my own essay, written from the other side of college after things have mostly turned out alright: "Why I Am Still An English Teacher." Just as my classes were thinking up small stories to illustrate how compassionate or curious they were, I was mining my years in the classroom for reasons why I'd returned that fall. For years, I admitted, I held my profession at arm's length, uncertain I really was a teacher. I thought I was more a writer. I was waiting to be more a writer.

But what happened, I explained, is that I practiced teaching day after day after day and became a good teacher. What happened is we moved abroad and teaching was my job. What happened is I found enough joy in the classroom to stay. As I wrote my essay and then modeled expansion and cuts with my classes, I thought how much becoming a teacher mirrors the writing process. So much messy work at the start. A few gorgeous images. But over the academic years, smoother transitions and more hearty middle paragraphs, perhaps even a bold imitation of another's style.

At the third revision of my post-college-career-acceptance essay, I almost believed teaching in the Middle East was exactly what I was supposed to be doing. As the year went on— waking up tired, running treadmill miles, negotiating traffic with kids in the backseat and opening the door to first period—I occasionally returned to that question of why I'm still an English teacher. I wasn't unhappy, but I wasn't sure either. I felt like my seniors. They were making big decisions and sometimes asked my opinion. I assured one class they would be okay, wherever they landed, eventually, maybe. They wanted to know how I chose my college. So I told them I went to a university that promised a scholarship, supposing I'd transfer after a year or two, but instead I studied English which led to me choosing a teaching certification which then led to me wandering from Wisconsin to Colombia to Kuwait. "See," I said, "it turns out okay." We laughed.

No choice is inconsequential. That's a terrifying thought for an eighteen year old. It's a terrifying thought for a thirty-six year old. I saw parallels between my seniors learning who they were and what they wanted next, and my own questions of why I was in the Middle East and what I was doing with my piles of notebooks and files of finished poetry and narrative pieces. Each of us went on with the year. Students shared rejections and acceptances. I took a writing workshop and renewed my teaching contract. Each of us started to see the shape of who we are, again.

Watching my seniors sort out their futures pointed me to mine. I accepted: I am a teacher and writer. More than that, though, I sensed the culmination of half a dozen years fighting to enjoy who I am, where I am. Last year when my daughter and son would come to my classroom after school I'd pull them to me, breathe their shampoo and sweat, kiss their foreheads and think, "Please don't take this away from me." Last year I felt my body settle into its shape. I worked on my writing with a trust that one day it lands for you to read. When I pray for my kids, I ask God that they grow into who they are. That was the gift of last year, that I grew more into who I am.

Knowing better who I am is in part knowing who I am not. As my seniors were dreaming new dreams I was letting go of old dreams. I was embarrassed. I measured so much of myself against first fantasies of adulthood, farfetched high school dreams. I am not a photojournalist covering conflict. I am not fashionable. I am not an Olympic distance runner. I am not rich. I am not single. I am not given to a month in Ireland each summer. I wondered what my seniors expected of their adulthood. They talked of engineering, business, medicine and law. They talked of London, Dubai, Boston, and LA. They talked of returning to Kuwait. But they cannot do all the things in their minds and they know it but they don't really know it yet.

One day my seniors will wake to letting go of the corporation or property or body. They will look and walk more like who they are. They will be new in unexpected ways, discovering a language or partner in their twenties, finding a paintbrush or cello in their thirties. They will wear marriage, parenthood, singleness. One day they will feel the weight of loss. But I hope that one day they will also wear their body, heart, mind, and spirit like they fit.

When June arrived I wasn't ready to say goodbye to my seniors. At the senior night and again at the senior breakfast and finally at the commencement ceremony, I kept thinking of things I wanted to say or wish or hope for my students. That class was witness to my understanding I can be a teacher and writer, practicing both with hope. The people you're near the moment you see or accept or embrace an important truth matter. After nine years abroad, I was over heartbreak. And they had helped me overcome it.

To be a teacher and an expat is to say goodbye a thousand times. More. My husband taped a map to the wall and sometimes I look at the pastel colors of countries and think of my friends as little dots there and there and there. I measure the space between us. The first few years in Kuwait I cried when close friends left, looking out my apartment window at the Gulf, already knowing the greater loss: that we wouldn't keep in touch past occasional email or Facebook likes, that our witness to one another's growth in faith or motherhood wouldn't continue over a coffee or on a walk. Then for a few years I didn't cry very much, perhaps accepting the greater loss. But last year my heart cut on the understanding I can't keep any of this and while I was sad to see my seniors graduate, I was sadder at the many future goodbyes I choose as a teacher and expat.

Now I have a new group of seniors who are as lovely as the last. We learn together. Sometimes I think of one of my seniors from last year, wonder how they are doing in winter weather or if they are still writing, but I don't yet feel the deep sorrow of June. Maybe I'll get to see who they are in another decade or two. Maybe they'll get to see who I continue to become. Maybe we'll walk in lines that don't cross again. But that class matters to me. They were with me as I decided I can be this.

For my ASK 2016 seniors

Sarah Marslender, a native of Brodhead, Wisconsin, teaches in Kuwait. She has taught high school English, including creative writing, for 13 years, 4 in the US and 9 in Colombia and Kuwait.

THE PAPER CRANE
Maureen Wellbery

My teaching career of 33 years has had many defining moments, but none as memorable as what I experienced during my first international post in 2007. It involved a first grade student named Kubo, a blue paper crane, and myself, a teacher who had never journeyed so far from home. But before getting to Kubo, we must rewind the clock.

The date was January 9. The year was 2000. A new millennium...a new beginning. It was 5 a.m. in Orlando, Florida. Disney World was closed to everyone but the ten thousand people who showed up to complete a half marathon. I was shivering. Not just from the pre-dawn temperatures, but also from the thought that I would be running for thirteen point one miles through the Magic Kingdom. What was I thinking?

My children were grown and out of the house. One was getting married in a few months, one was engaged and the third was in grad school. I had trained for months but considering my age (over 50) and having little athletic ability, I was very nervous. Doubt began to creep in. I had never participated in <u>any</u> athletic competition, much less a long distance race. I was certain that everyone else was experienced and had been running all of their lives. Could I even finish?

I had one goal, one focus, and that was to finish what I had begun even if it didn't make sense, even if the odds were not in my favor. I had to prove it to myself. No one could help me cross the line…it was up to me.

I somehow never stopped running. My time was well short of amazing, but it didn't matter. I had set a goal and succeeded. And got a huge Donald Duck medal to boot.

Several years later, seven to be exact, I was not getting any younger, and neither were my kids. My three daughters were married with small children and I had moved to California with my second daughter to help take care of my new grandson. I worked locally as a reading and math specialist and a year later her family had their second child, a girl, and no more bedroom space for Nana. I returned to my home base in North Carolina and contemplated what to do next.

As time does not wait for anyone, I knew there was much more to this world that I wanted to see.

In 2007, I took another risk and signed a contract to work at the Korea International School just outside of Seoul. Just as they had before the half marathon, my nerves were frayed once again. Doubts crept in. Although my children and family were excited for me, they all thought my choice was unwise, and not just because I was leaving my five young grandchildren behind.

They assumed an Asian culture would not prove an easy transition after a lifetime in the US.

Pushing 60, I was going to live outside the U.S. for the first time. The place I was moving did not share my language, my sense of space (no spacious house and yard!), nor my comfort zone. My children and grandchildren wouldn't be there. In fact, nobody I knew lived there…in the whole country! It was going to be risky, but I knew I could do it. After all, I had already crossed one finish line. Why not another?

And that's how I met Kubo. My initial class of twenty first-graders was made up mostly of Koreans whose parents had lived overseas but moved back to Korea for their work. One major exception was a new student named Kubo. Kubo was very shy and spoke no English (the language of our class) or Korean (the language of his peers). He came from Japan and didn't mingle with the others, even at recess. I was very worried about him but understood that children need time to transition to a new culture, a new school, and new friends.

One of the highlights of teaching first grade that year was watching the children work with small and large pieces of paper during our art time together. I was amazed at what the students could produce and came to appreciate how they loved origami. They were all proud of their individual creations and we hung them throughout the room.

Teaching students of such a young age is a tremendous challenge. Each child needs to learn the basics of reading, writing, and more while also being in an environment that encourages healthy social and emotional growth. At the same time, children should be encouraged to reach their potential and occasionally "reach for the stars." There are many ways to do this, but one of the methods I use is to share my own personal experiences. I tell each class of the doubt and worries I had with my half marathon. I now started doing the same for my move to Korea. That not only can you dream, you can also achieve.

I didn't know if those stories helped Kubo at the time. I was just trying to help him become comfortable academically, socially, and personally. I spoke to him gently every day but wasn't sure how much he understood. I just hoped that things would eventually work out.

The end of the year seemed to come soon after it started. I looked at the calendar and empirically knew that the months from August to June had passed, but still it did not seem possible. The students and I, in the midst of our excitement for the upcoming summer vacation (their excitement related to sleeping in and playing all summer, mine for returning to the US to see my family and pre-Korea friends), were busy signing autograph books. In addition to thinking about the upcoming summer, my mind was also filled with thoughts of cleaning the room, taking down bulletin boards, and packing up for the following year. I was so absorbed in my thoughts, yet I continued to sign books and wish each student a great summer and good luck in second grade.

When I looked up to smile at the next student I saw Kubo. He had no book to sign and his hands were behind his back. I waited and he slowly brought out his closed, right fist and brought it to my face. As he carefully unfolded his hand I saw a tiny, yet beautifully folded, blue crane. I thanked him for such a lovely creation and went to place it on my desk alongside cards other students had made. He looked upset and said, "No, please open it." I wondered what could possibly be inside. Slowly, carefully, I separated the folds of the crane. I then understood what he wanted me to see. In very small print Kubo had written a message in pencil: "Thank you for teaching us to dream."

I was speechless. Seconds passed where I could not respond. Emotions overwhelmed me. Kubo <u>had</u> heard. He <u>had</u> understood. Out of the few hundred students that had heard my story of overcoming challenges, Kubo was the only one who actually took the time to demonstrate, through origami no less, what it meant to him. Had I not moved to Korea, I would have never experienced this affirmation.

The joy I felt crossing the finish line of the half marathon was surpassed, half a world away and almost a decade later, by the words of a student crossing his own finish line.

It was a moment I will never forget.

"Every great dream begins with a dreamer. Always remember you have within you the strength, the patience, and the passion to reach for the stars…to change the world." *Harriet Tubman*

Maureen Wellbery, a native of Plainview, New York, teaches in Asheville, NC. She has taught in elementary schools for 33 years, 26 in the US and 7 in South Korea and Lithuania.

WHERE THEY'RE FROM
Kristi Dahlstrom

"Where are you from?" It is approximately the third question
we ask each other. Unless we've found something interesting
in the answers to "What's your name?" and "What do you
do?," we move on to our backgrounds.

That college student might not have a major; that guy you meet
at church may have gotten laid off yesterday. Since not
everyone can be depended upon to have a college major, or
even a job, we ask for origins. Everyone is from *somewhere*.
Unless, of course, you're from *everywhere*.

"Do you want to come forward, Ms. Dahlstrom?" They've
asked me several times, affable and self-sacrificing, motioning
their sticks down to the other side of the concrete multi-
purpose court where we're playing. "Do you *want* to play
goalie?" No reply. "I'm fine here," I shrug.

With a scarf, a warm fleece jacket, and two orange cones marking the goal on either side of me, I truly am fine. Actually, I am better than fine. It can't be above freezing on this cloudless autumn morning at Black Forest Academy, a Christian international boarding school in Southwestern Germany. I'm playing ball hockey with my Canadian history class. We're going head-to-head with the geography class.

Their teacher, a Canadian, leads students from many countries including Russia, Korea, the Netherlands, and China. I am the lone American on my team, playing goalie for the Canadians.

It's only second period, but news of this match has circulated around the school already. I overheard it as I came in today.
"D'you hear about the hockey game?"
"Yeah, the Canadians are going to *win*, right?"
"For sure. They have to."
That's my team.

So, here we are, the score is 3-3 (primarily due to my inexperience as a goalie), and I'm loving every moment. We have three too many players, so the Canadians generously rotate themselves in and out. A Saskatchewan-born girl declares that she can't play because she has a mock job interview next period, but after only ten minutes of cheering from the sideline she enters the game. With gleeful laughter and mischievous grins, they intercept, pass, and steal the show as they move the ball puck up and up. They are *good* at this.

Geography Teacher and I are heroes for devoting class time to a hockey game, but I know I'm only a spectator today, simply taking up the space between two cones so that the real players can weave their intricate game across the court. The other team really isn't bad, either, but I'm overwhelmed by the sense of pride and ownership that the Canadians take in this game. I try to imagine a group of similar American teenagers playing baseball somewhere, but the analogy fades in translation.

One of the things I've loved about teaching this class, I realize, is that together we are uncovering where they're from. Or at least one of the places. The Canadians don't all claim to be from Canada, and maybe they never will. Some of our students have never lived for extended periods in the country of their passports.

Yet as I watch them play hockey together, I realize that this is more important than just a morning of playing in the cold. Though we joke about it often, I can't really take them on a field trip to Canada, but we can play hockey. The majority of students at Black Forest Academy are the children of missionaries serving all around the Eastern Hemisphere. They may have been born in a place they've never lived, and may have moved more often than they've had birthdays. They don't know what it is to be "from" somewhere, so they answer that third question with a sigh of frustration.

In international schools, we often talk about what it means to be anchored to something outside nationality or home address. How 'home' isn't a specific building and how 'nations' are bigger than their borders. We talk about being at home in God's will or safe in the communities of family and friends, no matter how fleeting they may be.

I love it that our students are from everywhere, that they often claim several countries rather than one when asked to identify their origins. That's what I like about Black Forest Academy— the complex, international roots that link us to every corner of the world.

Today, however, I love that my Canadians are playing hockey—some of them for the first time, some for the hundredth—and that I get to experience 'from-ness' with them, if only for an hour.

Kristi Dahlstrom, a native of Seattle, Washington, teaches in southwestern Germany. She has taught high school humanities for 10 years, 4 in the US and 6 in Germany.

TO LEAVE OR NOT TO LEAVE?
Kevin A. Duncan

Two years can feel like an eternity. Staring at my first international contract in February 2006, I wasn't sure if I was shivering from the Iowa cold or from the nerves of having to sign on the dotted line. If I was going to pull the trigger and commit to teaching overseas, it would require a minimum twenty-four month stint away from the comforts of home.

Job fairs are a rollercoaster ride. Before arriving in Cedar Falls, I was hoping to spend the next two years of my life in Vietnam. By lunchtime of the first day, I was fairly confident the next two years would find me in the Philippines. When I laid down for the night after several interviews, I was trying to figure out how often I'd be flying back to the US from my likely home in Tanzania. 18 hours later, I had signed a two-year contract to teach in Costa Rica.

Costa Rica wasn't on my radar. But it was for everyone else who joined me: The couple who had met on a plane to Costa Rica seven years prior. The Katrina refugees, newlyweds moving south for a 2-year adventure while waiting for their beloved NOLA to be rebuilt. The guy who left his dream of playing drums to be with his Costa Rican girlfriend. And all the others. Turns out I was the only new teacher that year that hadn't already contacted the school before the job fair hoping to find gainful employment in the land of *pura vida*.

This international teaching thing was going to be awesome— two years in Costa Rica, then two years somewhere else, let's say South America, then eventually to Asia, Africa, then off to Europe. In 10 years, I would have lived in every corner of the world. Then, just like working a 500-piece puzzle, I would spend the next 20 years filling in the gaps inside the corners. If things really were amazing, I might stay in one spot for three or even four years. The whole world, not just one city or country, was my oyster.

School started, and it didn't take me long to realize I wasn't in Kansas (or the US) anymore. When some new coworkers and I were eating at Henry's, a local bar and grill, for the first time, we bumped into a grade 11 student. It made sense to ask him for a recommendation. Thinking I was going to hear something along the lines of "cheeseburger" or "quesadilla," it threw me for a loop when he said "the margaritas here are amazing." A genuine recommendation, not one trying to elicit a reaction. He was just helping out.

The unique experiences continued. I had my first ever student teacher, a former cop from L.A. who decided to follow in his father's teaching footsteps. After observing me for two weeks, it was time for Mr. B. to take over the class. I looked on the whiteboard at his brand new classroom rules and said, "Maybe you don't want to have #6." "No, I like it…I'm going to keep it." "I'm pretty sure that's not a good idea." "It'll be good."

Hours later, I heard "mooooo" and "bok-bok-bok" for the first time all school year. Rule #6? *No animal noises.*

There was never a dull moment. Could it be like this in other countries and at other schools?

"Don't leave, Mr. Duncan." Walking up the stairs each morning to my third-floor classroom, one of only two rooms in the whole school with the best view of the Costa Rican Central Valley, I'd often pass Kim Kim. Kim was her surname and Kim was her Western name. "Kim squared" was often the early bird, arriving a good 30 minutes before her peers. It was December of my second year, and it was nearing time to make a decision. Would I stay for a third? In international schools, decisions for the next August are often made nine months in advance. This particular year, due to some unique circumstances, my cohort was lucky enough to be able to decide super late...we could decide *seven* months early. "Kims" knew crunch time was coming. My childhood best friend from small town Tennessee happened to be getting married half a world away in Bali just one day before the international school job fair in Bangkok was to commence. I could double dip: wedding and job fair.

There were plenty of reasons to leave. The fact that we foreign teachers unknowingly didn't have health insurance for six weeks and were assured *afterwards* by the school director that "If anything catastrophic would have happened, the owner would have taken care of it." Quite comforting to know. The fact that the school was a for-profit entity where sometimes the bottom line took precedent over delivering the best possible education. The fact that while the pay was impressive for Central American schools, it was a fraction of what one could earn teaching in Asia or the Middle East. If I later decided to stay beyond 4 or 5 years, I would be moved to "local hire" status where my salary would be cut in half, housing would no longer be free, and my foreign health

insurance would exit stage left. The fact that some of my
closest friends were moving to their next opportunities. The
fact that the world was still my oyster.

But there were also plenty of reasons to stay. Some of them are
true no matter where one teaches internationally—it's nice
already knowing how to get photocopies made, where to get a
haircut, that your favorite restaurant's owner knows you by
name. Then there were also reasons specific to Costa Rica. I
could be at a beach, mountain, or a rain forest in just a few
hours. The best rotisserie chicken place in the world was right
around the corner. But more importantly, the people I knew
already felt like family in just 16 months of knowing them. My
roommates from the past two years were sticking around, as
were other close friends from my teaching "pledge class."
Next year's graduates also held a special place in my heart—I
had taught (or attempted to teach) them all history two years
prior and had led them on two experiential ed trips in remote
parts of the country. Kings of hustle and teamwork Umberto,
Robby, Gommert, and Jack were about to be the senior leaders
on the basketball team I coached. Future graduates in the class
behind them were also an awesome bunch that sometimes
even laughed at my jokes. Many of them would take my Econ
class as juniors and my AP World History class as seniors. Why
would I leave those relationships behind?

I also wanted to leave a legacy. But that's hard to do without
staying in one place for a long time. The week that I wrote this
story, a teacher who taught at my high school in Columbia,
Tennessee for over three decades passed away. Hundreds and
hundreds of people filled a gymnasium for his memorial
service. He left a legacy. He and other teachers had been at that
school so long they taught kids of former students. I, on the
other hand, had barely been in Costa Rica long enough to have
a cup of coffee. Actually, not even that long. I didn't have my
first cup of coffee until eight years later.

Therein lies the rub.

Like many things in life, it's impossible to have it all. The benefits of being a fixture in one place contrast with the benefits of having life experiences in a variety of locales. Each scenario can be helpful in teaching students both content and life lessons. The familiarity with a country and the relationships you develop are invaluable. But so are the cultural opportunities and new relationships that await you at your next stop. There is no perfect time to leave.

Arriving post-Bali wedding at the job fair in hot and humid Bangkok, two years after the frigid few days in Iowa, I started interviewing again. Instead of two years feeling like forever, two years now seemed like a flash in the pan. If I did decide to move on from Costa Rica, I hoped that I'd only be "2 and out" just this one time. A longer tenure may not ensure a lasting legacy, but at least it would delay the time before having to find a new barber. I started the job fair by emailing my family and friends the percent chance of either decision—50% stay, 50% go. Two days later, I was loosening my tie, listening to Rihanna's "Umbrella," and looking down at my freshly signed contract with a school in South Korea. I didn't honor Kim Kim's "Don't go" request, but I unexpectedly was heading to her home country. Once again, I committed to teach in a country not on my radar. Five years later, I would rediscover just how hard it can be to leave…again.

Kevin A. Duncan, a native of Columbia, Tennessee, teaches in Guangzhou, China. He has taught high school social studies for 15 years, 4 in the US and 11 in Costa Rica, South Korea, and China.

IN IT FOR THE LONG HAUL
Dave Archer

Yara approached the microphone, step after timid step, looking out toward one thousand anxious faces. Hands by her side, she inhaled deeply, breathing heavily into the microphone and producing a loud whoosh of air through the speakers. She had never spoken into a microphone before. The audience sat still, waiting for the assembly to begin while her parents held each other off to the side of the stage. My students rocked and fidgeted in their seats. And I, having witnessed such a remarkable transformation in a young person, closed my eyes and prayed for her success. The moment stretched for far too long. We were sure she wouldn't speak, and then she did. "My name is Yara. Welcome to 5B's morning meeting."

In 2009, I began my first teaching job at one of Kuwait's top international schools. Like every first-year teacher I was stressed to the teeth trying to find my way through mountains of grading and lesson plans while wondering how to create a community with my students and their parents. Unlike most first-year teachers I was 6,000 miles from home in one of the driest places on Earth, both in atmosphere and lack of alcohol, in a culture wrought with super wealth that trickled into every aspect of my students' lives. A ten-year-old's sense of the world is already hard enough to understand. Add the complexity of inherited oil money to the equation, and it becomes even more tricky. Compound all that with the fact that the only three boxes of personal items I shipped overseas to make Kuwait feel like home had gotten lost in the mail, and it was easy to understand how the first few months were riddled with 'What did I get myself into?' moments. When I was down in the dumps my first semester, I wondered if I had given up my dream of becoming a travel writer too soon. I knew I wanted to be living abroad but maybe I had rushed into teaching too quickly. Hell, maybe I had rushed going abroad too quickly.

There were so many ups and down in my first six months in Kuwait that I was sure I'd be heading back to Boston after my two-year contract ended. I dealt with a fair amount of homesickness and spent too much time on Facebook following the lives of my friends in the States. But I tried to remain positive and finally found a routine, a rapport, and even a balance between my professional and personal life. I learned how to play ultimate frisbee and joined a basketball league on the weekends. I brewed beer and ordered black market rum made from dates. I taught reading to 24 kids at a time with ability levels ranging from kindergarten to 7th grade. I knew when my recess duty was and how long it took to walk my class to their specialists. I even figured out a decent pace to walk at which I wouldn't sweat too much on the 100+ degree days.

By February I was ready to take on a new challenge: tutoring. Tutoring was encouraged in Kuwait and if you were able to do it often, you could really pull in quite a few extra dinars to pad your bank account. I asked my vice principal if anyone was looking for a tutor; he gave me the name of a 3rd grade student named Yara. Yara's parents wanted her to get help in all her subjects, especially math, but her real issue, according to the VP, was that she wouldn't speak at school. Yara was a selective mute. In five years, not one teacher had heard her speak.

My first thought was, "Yara should be at a school that supported students with learning disabilities because no one on our staff specialized in student support." My second thought was, "Why would she tell me anything? I'm 6'7" with a big red beard. This little girl is going to be terrified of me!"

Nonetheless I took the job. I was looking for a challenge and Yara would certainly be that. I could at least help with homework, and her teacher was my good friend so I expected whatever I couldn't get out of Yara about the goings on in her class, I could get from Joe.

The following Monday I was picked up after school by Naveen, Yara's friendly driver, and taken to her house. The mansion could have fit mine and my closest friends' houses inside with room to spare. Everything was wide open and gigantic. Enormous Persian rugs, floor cushions and sofas decorated the diwaniya, a place for men to gather after dinner. A dining room table was set with golden plates and silverware at each of the thirty seats. The kitchen was constructed for professional chefs and they had one on staff plus two nannies, Naveen, and another driver. The staff was still no match for the opulence of the mansion. All of them could have walked side by side up the four-story spiral staircase and still had room to spare.

Yara was in the playroom at her desk, flipping briskly through the pages of a Magic Treehouse volume, as if looking for her favorite line. I sat down with apprehension, taking in my surroundings and wondering how everything would pan out with this silent child. But before I could even say hello, Yara burst out with a string of questions so rapid fire that she was out of breath before I even had time to answer. "Do you like ice cream? Do you know my teacher? Do you like Kuwait? Do you read Magic Treehouse books? I don't like fish, do you like fish?"

I was dumbfounded. She was a chatterbox! She couldn't get a whisper out at school but had so much to say that she couldn't stop talking once she got home. Her English was clearly behind her 3rd grade peers which was no surprise, but she strung her sentences together clearly enough to get her point across and was smarter than she was able to demonstrate in class. As happy as I was to hear her speak I also felt so sorry for her because she was overcome by such extreme anxiety that she couldn't communicate with anyone at school. She ran around at recess with her classmates, kicking the soccer ball or playing tag, but she could never share in lunch conversation. She went through class routines, having no difficulty reading rules or directions, but she couldn't bring herself to ask even the simplest of questions out loud. Joe was one of the most compassionate and welcoming teachers I'd ever met. He cared so deeply for each student and helped everyone shine in their own light, but even he could not put Yara's mind at ease enough for her to recognize her classroom as a safe space. The power of the mind is remarkable. Even as adults we often fail to grasp the complexities of our own thoughts and decision making. But for children whose academic and social lives are in such early stages, the limitations must be so much more confusing. Yara had an undiagnosed disability that impacted her daily school life and learning, and this eventually became too much for the school to handle.

I worked with Yara twice a week for the remainder of the school year. Her grades went up slightly as she was able to understand assessment expectations and study the correct information. Ultimately however, she was asked to leave the school because she still could not perform her daily tasks. The principal made a deal with her parents, that if she transferred schools for 4th grade, raised her grades and started speaking in class, then she could return for 5th and move onto middle school with us. I spoke with her parents about this often but ultimately agreed with my principal and our school counselor that it might be best to try a new environment for a year. Yara could develop her language skills in a place where no one knew her limitations, and return to us with a confidence and understanding of her ability.

As she and I continued to work on Monday and Wednesday afternoons, she gained confidence in her new classroom at a different international school, just as we had hoped. Her writing, math, and reading all improved and our relationship grew stronger. I recognized how hard I could push before she gave up, and when I could elicit more complete responses to my questions. I continued teaching 5th grade and left the homesickness behind, settling in fully to my Kuwaiti lifestyle, even signing on for a third year. During orientation at the start of year three I received my class list and there, third from the top, was Yara. She requested my class out of the six available teachers, bravely returning to her old environment of discomfort to be my student.

One of the elements of my classroom that I attribute my community building to is the morning meeting. It offers a platform for students to feel safe among one another and gives them an opportunity to greet, share, and interact in a quick succession of activities. Our school adopted this practice during my last year in Kuwait and, to provide leadership opportunities, asked each 5th grade class to lead an all-school morning meeting on the soccer field at some point in the year.

We practiced and practiced, making sure each word added positively to our assembly. My class was small that year, just 17 students, giving everyone an equal opportunity to shine on stage. But we all had a concern for Yara. She now spoke in class every day, but she was still feeling some of her old insecurities from 3rd grade. Yara was shy at best, but other days she would find it difficult to say much of anything. Our bond was different now; I was unable to tutor my own students, so the quiet moments we shared during lunch at her home disappeared. I was fearful that Yara might slip back fully to her old ways. Still, she seemed optimistic approaching the time for our assembly. We had a silly greeting to teach the audience, some jokes to tell, and plans for Hamad, Ali, and Talib, the three breakdancers from our class, to bust a few moves. I tried my best to stay out of the students' way as they chose roles and wrote scripts, especially when it was determined that Yara would be first to speak. She was initially excited at being chosen for the opening lines, but I could see the feeling recede the more we rehearsed.

On the morning of our big day, the elementary students started filing in from the parking lot. They congregated with their classes in lines on the field, facing the stage elevated before them. The mics and speakers on, my students were anxious for the show to begin as they sat in their spots facing the crowd. Our principal came to the mic and welcomed the families and students to the school, then gave me the nod to begin. I in turn looked to Yara and she approached the stand.

"My name is Yara. Welcome to 5B's morning meeting. We have a great show for you and we hope you enjoy it." Her voice didn't waver. She didn't mumble or move from side to side. She spoke with confidence in front of one thousand people and it was all I could do not to cry. When she finished her lines she turned to go back to her chair. Her smile was so big and proud that a tear or two did escape. Yara had found an ability buried deep within herself and with determination, allowed it to break free.

People outside (and sometimes in) the international teaching world often shake their heads when I mention living in Kuwait for three years. They don't understand why a person would choose to live in a place that different from home and, to be honest, I often have difficulty finding many positives that outweigh the negatives from my time spent there. But I do have the experience with Yara and the confidence I was able to help her realize. I have the experience of difficulties overcome through determination and the need to succeed for the sake of someone else. I have the memory of her confidence manifesting itself in those brief lines of our all-school morning meeting. Having tutored and taught Yara I gained a love for teaching that I hope all teachers experience at some point in their careers. I realized after leaving Kuwait that I was in this for the long haul. I was a teacher and I would be one for the rest of my life. To provide a young person with such confidence and open their eyes to their own possibilities gives me the deepest sense of satisfaction I could ask for. I am fortunate to love what I do, and I absolutely love being a teacher.

Dave Archer, a native of Beverly, Massachusetts, teaches in Seongnam, South Korea. He has taught 5th grade for 8 years in Kuwait and South Korea.

V. TRAVELING OVERSEAS

GRANNIES IN MOROCCO
Carmel Pezzullo

At one point or another, when traveling, we all find ourselves
in situations we never thought we would be in. Many times
these are fun new adventures where we experience food,
people, and cultural moments that are out of our comfort
zones in the best way. We do things we have never done
before or wouldn't normally do. But what about the times
when you find yourself in these situations in a negative way? A
cultural moment forces you to do something you never
thought you would do and leaves you asking yourself, "How
did I get here?" While traveling in Morocco, I found myself in
one of those cultural situations.

My friend Sandra and I were in Fez, and after spending some
time exploring the medinas, we decided to head back to our
hotel for a much needed shower and rest. The sky was quickly
darkening and our feet had done their good deeds for the day.
It was time to get a taxi. In my very limited French, I braved

asking one of the million residents if there was a place where we could find one. He sent us down a questionable alleyway, the kind your mother wants you to avoid. When we emerged from the alley we found that there wasn't actually a taxi stand but, instead, a derelict, abandoned lot. Milling around this lot was a large group of women aged 60 to 80. These sweet grannies had arms full of shopping bags and talked excitedly to one another in Arabic. Apparently we had decided to head home at the exact same time Morocco's third generation had finished their Sunday night grocery shopping. Mixed in the crowd was a small group of preteen boys who definitely seemed out of place. There was a strange vibe in the parking lot, like everyone was waiting for something, although nothing seemed to be happening.

We slowly walked around to try to figure out what was going on. Nobody was standing in any kind of line, just in a huge crowd. Sandra and I looked at each other, realizing that obviously we misunderstood the directions and were clearly in the wrong place. Just as we were about to retrace our steps, a taxi came speeding around the corner, flying into the vacant lot. What happened next played out in slow motion before our unbelieving eyes. The grannies, who had been milling around and chatting, became serious. Their faces turned to stone; their thick eyebrows furrowed in concentration. As the taxi got closer, the sweet little grannies turned into professional wrestlers, and a war cry of noise and shouting began. Their white plastic bags, filled with a mixture of packaged mini-cakes and lamb chops, turned into weapons. Their arms were wielding those bags like a ninja holds nunchucks. Elbows were being thrown. Frail hands shoved other women with a herculean-like force, grannies tackling other grannies like rugby players as they all fought to reach the cab. Amongst the women, I saw a young boy fling his body onto a taxi as it came speeding in, grasping onto the hood for dear life until the taxi came to a halting stop. Moments later, the taxi sped away from the craziness with two triumphant grannies in the back and the boy running alongside it with his arm inside, getting it out from the window just before the taxi reached highway speed and disappeared into the opposite alleyway.

I stood there in shock, my mouth hung open, as I tried to make sense of the frenzied scene around me. I couldn't believe what I had just witnessed. Just as I was trying to understand exactly what had happened and before I even said a word to Sandra, another taxi came flying into the lot and the last scene was replayed. A boy jumped on a car, grannies fought, a few won, and everyone else started to wait for their next chance.

After watching 5 more taxis enter and leave the lot in the exact same fashion, we understood that we had to figure out a plan. Sandra and I talked about going elsewhere to find our way back, but due to our lack of knowledge of the city and the late hour, we determined that it was not a viable option. "Maybe we can just wait out the grannies?" I said to Sandra with a hopeful look. But as we looked around, we realized that more women kept piling into the lot, far more than the number of taxis that were arriving. The crowd was multiplying; we were further away from leaving than when we arrived. There was no telling when this would end.

After the 10th taxi, a dark realization set in. We knew deep down, much to our chagrin, that it was an eat or be eaten situation. Sandra and I would have to do something we never would have imagined ourselves doing even five minutes prior. The only way out was to take down the grannies.

We took a deep breath, gave each other a reassuring look, and threw ourselves into the crowd, clawing our way as close to the front as possible. We heard the screech of tires, looked to the heavens, held our breath and prayed that this would turn out OK. When the next taxi came rearing in, we realized very quickly that we had underestimated the strength of these women. I tumbled, lost in a sea of flabby arms and large bosoms. Before we knew it, the taxi had been won over by only one granny and was already speeding out the other side.

We lost the next two taxis in the same fashion. Exhausted and bruised, we were no closer to the comfort of our hotel. Sandra and I needed help. It was time, this fourth and final round, to touch the ground outside of the ring, to call on a teammate to enter on our behalf…a 12-year-old boy. I signaled him to come closer and uttered one word: "Help." He quickly deduced that a foreigner would pay much more than any local grandmother and gladly agreed to jump in the ring.

The sound of the engine and brakes had us in the starting position. Our arms were out to the side, our knees bent, ready to sprint forward. The taxi came speeding in and the boy was on the hood of that car before I knew it. Still in the starting position, I felt the pushing beginning and knew that my body weight alone was no match. I started wildly throwing my elbows, not really sure where they were landing. I connected with stomachs, backs, sides, and, at one point, a cheekbone. I didn't care. I was yelling out my own war cry at this point as I shoved the grannies aside. Our boy climbed onto the roof of the car to access the door. We continued through the gauntlet until somehow we managed to throw ourselves in—body slam style—right as the door closed. "We did it!" Sandra and I cried out as we laid on top of each other across the back of the cab. As the taxi sped away, we caught our breath and untangled ourselves.

It suddenly occurred to us that we hadn't paid the boy. We begged the driver to stop, but either he didn't speak French or he had blocked that word from his mind. The way he was driving, it was likely the latter. Through the back window, we saw the young boy who had just been swindled by some tourists grow smaller and smaller until the car found its way to the alley.

The triumph of the moment quickly faded and Sandra and I exchanged guilty looks. What had we just done? Did we really just resort to violent measures against the elderly to get a cab? Had we really just denied payment to a kid who helped us? The truth had set in, but a more important question emerged: "What would we have done different?" Of course we didn't want to do any of those things, but the circumstances were so unique that it felt right at the time. But they felt way wrong after. We were just small drops of water in a sea of people trying to get the same thing. What was unnatural for us seemed like standard practice for so many. Maybe we were OK.

There is an old travel saying, "When in Rome, do as the Romans do." I had always thought of that as a light-hearted phrase, meant to highlight the fun things you do while in other countries like eat too much of a certain food or participate in a fun cultural dance. But Morocco changed that for me. Now, when I hear that phrase, I know that "do as the Romans do" might also mean "elbow a granny in the face."

Carmel Pezzullo, a native of Melbourne, Australia, teaches in Shanghai, China. She has taught in elementary schools for 10 years, 2 in Australia and 8 in Spain, Colombia, and China.

THE OTHER SIDE
Norman Schwagler

I hate Afghans. No, not the people. Afghan hounds. They're snooty and mean…everything you don't want in a dog. The one I met during my early days in Seattle was named *Chaucer*. I know, not pretentious at all. The *very first* night I moved in to my new place, Chaucer left a gift for me outside my bedroom door, something akin to a plate of *welcome to the neighborhood* brownies one might receive from the sweet old lady across the street, but not exactly.

Thinking back to that period in my life, Chaucer's hospitality is one memory that floats to the top, encapsulating how I felt during the early part of my twenties when I had first moved to Seattle. Restless, miserable, not fitting in, unwanted, knowing I wanted more, but not sure how to get it.

Life seemed a constant stream of movement and struggles. I wrote poems in coffee shops about how my own American

Dream was *slipping away*. I sported ridiculous sideburns and a chain wallet. I applied to the Peace Corps, painted houses, delivered pizzas, and even delivered phone books. I yearned to do something bigger than myself, chase a dream as it were.

****

Fifty Thai kids, sweating, but collectively not nearly as much as the giant standing in front of them, are hoping that I can teach them anything. Preferably involving English. This classroom is choked with chalk dust somewhere on the outskirts of Bangkok. Way on the outskirts. The last time I was in a classroom myself was years ago, studying Political Science. I have no formal training in teaching. I have no sleep (after arriving in the country just 6 hours prior). I have no idea what to say back to the 100 eyes staring at me. But I do have that dream. And I'm definitely, definitely doing something bigger than myself. "Hello. My name is Mr. Norman. I like clocks."

Fifty kids leave, fifty more kids arrive. Stop, rinse, repeat. Many more times. I teach 800 kids a week.

At the end of each day, the students pack up and go to their homes. As the first and only foreigner teaching at that school, I'm housed in a converted classroom on the school grounds, sort of like a caged albino tiger. My only roommates now are the hungry mosquitoes who visit me in the early morning hours and, not to be left out lest I hurt their feelings, the cockroaches the size of Milky Way candy bars. I also have, for lack of a better term, a man-servant who wakes me up and washes my clothes in a big plastic bowl.

My bathroom in the new digs is not, shall we say, pristine. A few weeks after arriving, the toilet becomes so clogged and full of methane gas that when I throw a match in it to mask the smell, a flame shoots three feet in the air. Thankfully, no face, limbs, or eyebrows are damaged. Nor are the sideburns…they didn't make the trip to Thailand. I doubt they would have cleared customs.

Each time the 100 Thai eyes stare back at me, I get a little better at teaching. I start to figure out a few things here and their. There English is slowly improving. But nowhere near good enough to know the difference between their and there.

At the time, I didn't know anything about international schools. I didn't know that you can teach overseas without having insects for roommates or fires in your toilet. I didn't know that teaching 800 kids a week was WAY more than most people teach in several years. I didn't know that you could have a multiple week orientation to get adjusted to the country and prepared to teach in the school. I didn't know that you could actually save money teaching internationally. I didn't know that international school teachers, who loathe to be compared to lowly English teachers, bristle when people ask them *"Do you teach English?"* "No, I teach science… *in English."* Snobs.

Seven weeks in, I know I made the right decision to leave Seattle and try something new, but perhaps this teaching thing is not for me. I'm contemplating throwing in the towel but know that I mustn't. I can't go back to delivering phone books. That's why this mid-term break, my first one, is so needed. Sure, I need to recharge my batteries but, more importantly, I am excited to try out my new vocation. In my mind, it's a hell of a lot sexier and a stretch more daring than teaching: travel writing.

Documenting a 10-day bicycle trip through Laos is the perfect opportunity, I decide, to kick-start my budding literary career. Before leaving, I contact my friends in Seattle who run a website called "The Mountain Zone." They agree to publish my still unwritten story. Their website may need a bigger server after my post, I'm thinking. Everyone will want to read the hilarious yet poignant tale where the author traverses unexplored Laotian byways, conversing with remote villagers and uncovering majestic, unexplored wonders of the Far East.

I show up to Bangkok's Hua Lamphong train station a few hours early for the overnight ride to Khon Kaen, a 24-hour stopover where I'll visit my friend before crossing the border into Laos. My early arrival to the station is directly correlated with my unawareness of just how long it will take the bike to be stored safely and securely on the train. 30 minutes? 1 hour? 1 and ½ hours? Will there be forms to fill out? After about 15 seconds of bureaucratic 'red tape,' i.e. handing Bank (his nickname, not his birth name) the equivalent of a 75 cent tip, my bike gets loaded on to the train, no questions asked. Bank ties the bike up to a railing in one of the front storage cars. I'm nervous…those wheels hold the key to my new dreams, my new identity, my new career. "Mai mee bpen ha!" No problem! It will be safe. Bank is confident. "You can bank on it!" he says…or at least that's how I like to remember it.

Shuffling back to my seat, I realize this is a very long train.

I pass the next few hours before bedtime contemplating my meal of cold fried rice and playing several rounds of an intense one-man game of "count the cockroaches." My six-foot frame contorts into the five-foot bed. I drift into an uneasy slumber.

I'm a bottle of Coke inside of a vending machine. My brain combines the absolutely frigid air conditioning of a 2nd class Thai train cabin, a neon light that's never switched off, and the cramped quarters of an upper sleeping berth. Rarely has a dream been so vivid. *Someone puts in 4 quarters. I fall from my perch to the bottom of the machine.* My eyes open.

People are scurrying about. The train is stopped. *How long has it been sitting here?*, I wonder. I scramble, strapping on my fanny pack and grabbing my backpack and bike helmet while wiping the sleep from my eyes. This high adventurer needs to get his ass in gear.

I exit the train, half-asleep, walking slowly towards the front to retrieve my bike. It's about 5 in the morning, still dark outside. The tropical heat feels so exotic to me. It's invigorating after my night in the vending machine. Every step makes me feel more human again, upright and moving.

The plan is coming together, I think, *step one of the journey. I've made it to Khon Kaen.* I keep walking towards the front of the train. Passengers are disembarking and workers are unloading luggage. I don't see my bike yet. "Mai mee bpen ha." No problem. I continue walking.

Scrreeeech!

The train lurches backward and then forwards. There is a sound, the hiss of brakes being released. The train starts moving. At this point, I am not even halfway to the front.

I quicken my pace, walking with the purpose of someone who is seeing yet another dream slip away. The stones beside the track are sharp and awkward to walk on. *Hiss, creak, moan.* The train is picking up speed at an alarming rate. I am running now, shouting to no one in particular to hold on. Wait! *Jakayan!* My bike!

The train has gone from a dead stop to 20km per hour in what seems like a matter of seconds. I am running full steam, realizing I need to make a decision—hop back on this thing or let it go.

The train's air conditioning is no match for this American's brief dash through the Thai heat. As sweat cascades down my face, I struggle to catch my breath, working my way through the aisles, trying to get to the front. Gone is the suave adventurer who mere hours ago had sauntered so gentlemanly through the carriages, fielding smiles from female admirers with a grace only a secret agent or fearless adventurer might muster. In his place is my old self, an awkward American spaz, donning a fanny pack, seeing his dreams of being a travel writer quashed before the adventure even began. I am thinking now this bike is gone forever.

Reaching the front of the train I communicate my problem. Well, I try to. After a few attempts using my broken Thai and a lot of hand gestures, the conductor finally understands. He radios back to the station and tells me...

My bike is waiting for me in Khoen Kaen. The larger items were unloaded on the other side of the train; the side I could not see.

Instant Nescafe never tasted so good. Like a little kid I am perched next to the driver in the engine compartment. We talk a bit. His voice quells my panic and I have to laugh at myself. The window is open. I look out as the sun begins to reluctantly break the horizon over the lush, green rice fields. I can't remember the last time I just sat and watched the sun rise. *This is you being a traveler,* I think to myself.

I stop in the next town, an hour north, buy a ticket and head back to Khon Kaen.

****

I finished the bike trip as planned, myself and bicycle intact. I wrote and published the article.

The moments that stuck with me? They were not the ones spent taking in majestic sites or experiencing exotic foods and culture as an intrepid traveler may encounter.

The moments that threaded their way into my memory and conscience were the ones of people.

The train conductor who clearly saw the humor in my predicament. The woman who rode alongside me that first morning as I left Vientiane, quietly chatting as we pedaled out of town, she on her way to school, me on my way to a big adventure. I recall the generosity of the monk who let me sleep on the temple floor in a small Lao town that had no hotels, and that morning being woken by the laughing and chatting old women braiding flowers into garlands that would be used as temple offerings.

I returned to my classroom in Thailand re-energized, ready to take on head first the challenges that still awaited. I completed my one-year contract and stayed even longer, discovering that there was something about teaching that I loved, something bigger than myself. The problems of inexperience, mosquitos, and too many students were still there, but I was learning how to manage and had also discovered a new-found joy being in the classroom and living overseas.

There, in my first few months living abroad, I realized that there is more than one side to every situation. What seem like insurmountable problems, when viewed from another angle, may just turn out to be the kind of opportunities and experiences that shape our lives. I would have never met the conductor or had the memory of watching the sun rise over the rice fields if I hadn't made the mistake of leaving my bike behind. Twenty years later I still struggle with my self-identity and insecurities, but it's nice to know *there's always another side to the train.*

Norman Schwagler, a native of Buffalo, New York, teaches in Guangzhou, China. He has taught middle school social studies and English for 17 years, 2 in the US and 15 in Thailand, South Korea, and China.

THE OPENING OF A MIND
Brian Lalor

"I was just about nineteen when I landed on their shore, with eyes big as headlights, like the thousands and thousands who came before. I was going to be something! Smiled at the man scrutinizing my face, as I walked down off of the gangway." The words of Paul Brady describe the familiar story of young Irish people emigrating from Ireland. Ever since the great potato famine in the 1800s, Irish men and women have been packing their bags for the U.S., the U.K. or 'Down Under' in Australia. For me, the journey was to Asia, where I was to be changed forever.

I grew up in the southern province of the Republic of Ireland. Where I come from, Dublin is considered West-Britain and no one goes north of the border. I would consider my hometown a Republican area. As young adults, we would go out every Friday night and listen to our favourite live bands play rebel music. These were ballads that glorified the IRA's struggle against Britain. We learned at a young age to hate anything to do with England or Protestantism. Even though there was a Protestant school and a number of churches in my town, I do not recall ever speaking to a Protestant before the year 2004, when I was 24 years old.

My old Irish language teacher, Paddy, instilled in us from a young age a great desire to travel. Instead of teaching Irish, he would invite speakers from all over the world to come and talk to us. He, himself, would travel regularly to the U.S. and Canada during the summers and play music. His stories and his invited speakers inspired me to travel as well.

My original plan was to get a construction job in Boston, but that idea ended after I did serious damage to my back playing rugby. The next best option was a one-year visa to Australia to get bar work. On the way, I decided to stop off and stay with "Mad Dave," my friend who lived in Jakarta.

When I landed in Jakarta, culture shock hit me big time. Everybody was staring at me and exclaiming, "Bule!," "foreigner" in Indonesian. Security guards carried batons and soldiers had AK-47s. Having to use a hole-in-the-ground toilet was a big shock. I wanted to return home. I could not communicate enough to even order food.

Mad Dave had to pull me out of the apartment and feed me. He was surprised at my behavior. I eventually ran out of money and needed to get a job. Construction or engineering were no longer options, so I tried my hand at teaching. It was through this first teaching job that I would meet Kristina, a woman who would change my life forever.

From the first day, I noticed something different about Kristina. There was a kind of peace and joy in her that I could not identify. She genuinely cared for me and all of her employees. She mentored me to be a kindergarten English teacher and I fell in love with the job. I felt so grateful for my job and for Kristina's mentoring; she set me up for success.

However, one day, and I write this with a tear in my eye, everything changed. I learned that Kristina was a Protestant! She was a part of the people I had learned to hate all my life. It reminded me of when my best friend at university came out of the closet, breaking down another deep-seated stereotype. Due to the love and care Kristina showed me, during this difficult time in my life, I began to understand that Protestants were people too. I can only imagine how crazy this sounds to people who do not understand my national context. But for an Irishman like me, this was truly groundbreaking.

After a year and a half in Indonesia, I traveled overland through Southeast Asia for about six weeks and decided to stop in Vietnam and see if I could find work there. I noticed that the care, peace, and joy that Kristina displayed was evident among other Protestants. I had already developed a great interest in religion, studying the Koran in Jakarta and spending time in a Buddhist monastery in Thailand. I even meditated regularly and was searching for enlightenment. Thus, I started attending an international fellowship in Hanoi to learn more about Christianity.

During this time, I was devastated when I realized that I could no longer play sports due to an injury while on tour with the Viet Celts Gaelic football team. I once again damaged my back and I was in pain every day. This also impacted my social life, a life which revolved around sports.

One day, while alone on the top floor of one of those tall, skinny Hanoi houses, I got on my knees and prayed to God for help. I knew it was only the kind of God that Kristina talked about that could help me in this situation. I was not healed physically on that day, and still struggle with the back pain, but something far more amazing happened. I became enlightened as the true light of Jesus Christ entered my spirit and I was flooded with the peace and joy that emanated from Kristina. It is very difficult to describe this experience, but I found myself waking up every morning after to check if it was real; I was delighted to find out that it was.

Thus, I became a Protestant. I began to love all peoples and religions. From Protestants to Pentecostals, Buddhists to Muslims, all prior stereotypes were smashed and I began to follow the saying, "Before you can take the splinter out of your neighbour's eye, take the log out of your own." I can only say that, indeed, there was a log taken out of my eye. That is my story of how, through international education, I not only learned to love those I hated, but I actually became a member of that group. My old teacher Paddy used to say "Travel is the university of life." How right he was.

Brian Lalor, a native of Munster, Ireland, teaches in Shaanxi, China. He is currently the Head of Primary at his school and has taught for 13 years in Vietnam, Indonesia, and China.

SPANISH SORPRESAS
Lynn Bilbrey

In the summer of 2011, a few years after my move from teaching in the metropolis of Puyallup, Washington to an actual metropolis known as Seoul, I decided to take a semi-solo summer trip to Europe—London, Amsterdam, and then to the Spanish cities of Salamanca, Barcelona, Valencia and Madrid. "Semi" because I planned to meet up with friends from university or Korea in each city. "Solo" because, even though I was meeting friends, this would still be the first time in my life I would ever be navigating around by myself, except for when I had studied abroad during my senior year in London. Being shy and an introvert by nature, I have never been someone who enjoys striking up conversations with strangers wherever I go. Also, I didn't see the thrill in being a spontaneous traveler...I only saw the potential for something to go wrong. I'm a detailed planner, an organizer, a pre-thinker; look in my bag at any time, whether traveling on the go or just going about daily life, and you will find a mini pharmacy for virtually any ailment or injury nestled inside a variety of snacks, tissues, hand sanitizer, and extra wet wipes. Because you never know.

London went without a hitch—smooth flights, easy rides on the tube, good times reconnecting with old friends. Amsterdam followed suit; not only was the city beautiful, my friends taught me the genius of grocery store food shopping over taking more expensive outings to restaurants and cafés. I was on a roll.

It was time to keep venturing further into uncharted territory. That step further was doing a very un-Lynn thing—not booking <u>all</u> of my transportation and accommodations for the Spanish leg of the trip. My only reservations were for flights in and out of Madrid and an apartment rental in Barcelona where I would meet up with Tim and Aysem, the teaching couple I'd just hung out with in Amsterdam.

I fell in love with Spain right away...the weather, amazing food, and random encounters with locals led to some unexpected, unplanned, and unforgettable moments. A random detour one afternoon with the friendly José, an elderly man around 70 with a full head of white hair, a white beard, and vibrant, kind eyes, ended up with me getting a personal tour of one of the best views of Salamanca from a virtually unknown lookout tower, complete with a little *baila de dos*, or dance for two, at the top with my new favorite Spanish septuagenarian. I had the best paella, the kind you have to reserve in advance, with *vino tinto* in an authentic local restaurant. Two great memories that were all part of this spontaneous Spanish summer. I was digging this go-with-the-flow travel style...it had been nothing but smooth sailing thus far. In Barcelona, that all changed.

It started when I, the *nuevo* Lynn, booked a last-minute flight from Salamanca to Barcelona via Madrid. I was supposed to meet the Barcelona apartment landlord around 11:00 p.m. to get the keys, but my flight from Madrid was delayed over an hour, putting me into Barcelona around midnight. At the Madrid airport, I scrounged together a few Euros and phoned (yes, pay phones still existed in 2011!) the landlord, a woman named "Biggie." "Sorry, I'm going to be late…" "No problem, Lynn, I will wait here," was the raspy reply on the other end. Relieved for the moment, I just hoped Tim and Aysem could find the place since I would no longer be arriving there first.

Being someone who prides herself on being prepared, and by that time a "world traveler," my pride took a hit when I realized I hadn't looked up how to actually get to this apartment from the Barcelona airport. I had no Barcelona city metro app, no map at all, and no directions from the apartment rental site to even give to a cab driver. Arriving just before midnight, I found myself following the rush of stragglers leaving the airport who were catching the last train out for the night. Saying a silent prayer and hoping for the best, I ran onto the train without even buying a ticket. It was a double decker, and for some reason even though the cars were virtually empty, I felt safer going upstairs and took a seat across from a blonde girl in her twenties. She and I were two of the only four people in the whole train car; the rest of the seats were empty.

Plopping down with my travel backpack still attached around my shoulders, I took out my trusty iPod touch and found the e-mail from Biggie…there was an address! (Relief numero uno) Still not having any clue where this train was headed or what part of Barcelona the apartment was in, I mustered up the nerve to approach the stranger across from me. In my shy Spanish I asked if she might know where I should get off to get to this address.

She looked up and glanced at the address for all of two seconds.

"Sure," she replied back in English. (Relief numero dos) "I think you can just get off in two stops, and from there get on a bus outside the station which will take you close to where you're going." I don't know if she was Spanish herself; her English hinted at some other European accent behind it, more Warsaw Pact than NATO. If it had been daylight, and had I not been so flustered and anxious, I would have maybe asked her where she was from and what she was doing in Barcelona. Maybe. The "I" in my INTJ may have had something to say about that or, more accurately, not to say.

Two stops later, I thanked my navigation guardian angel, and moments later found myself waving goodbye on the platform while watching the train slowly move away. Again, it's now just me and an address. I forgot what the bus number was. No matter…at that time the little shy, innocent, alone, vulnerable (and unprepared) girl in me took over and said "It's midnight, Lynn. You're by yourself in a foreign city. Just get there. It's taxi time." Seeing several taxis waiting outside the station, again a silent prayer went up to the travel gods that someone knew her way around Barcelona enough to point me in the right direction. However, being tired and flustered in the rush to 'just get there,' my Spanish failed me temporarily and instead of telling the driver number 79, I told him number 97. There was no 97. Looking back on it, I probably lucked out not knocking on some stranger's door, awakening them in the midst of their slumber to find some non-Spanish woman with a backpack who desperately could use a shower staring back at them. For their troubles, at least I could have offered them some sleeping pills from my bag because, well, you never know.

After a couple of wrong turns trying to find the apartment, I finally found myself outside the right building. While handing the driver a few wrinkled Euros, I heard a low, oddly-familiar husky voice to my right. "Lynn?"

There was "Biggie"…all five feet nothing and one hundred pounds of her, probably 45 years old if a day, with a short buzz cut of greying hair, wearing a faded tie-dye t-shirt and a denim mini skirt with a frayed hem. Cigarette in one hand, cell phone in the other.

"Biggie?" I asked, feeling equal parts amazed and weirdly comforted at the same time. Biggie had this instant vibe about her, one where you knew that nobody would dare mess with her, because Biggie would clearly Rough. You. Up.

"Sí, Lynn, glad you made it...your friends are already here, inside, upstairs. And your other friend was just here too."

"Oh really? That's great, I'm so sorry for being here so late, my flight was delayed and I didn't know the way and..........what other friend?!"

"Yes, the friends you meet here, they are upstairs now. But your other friend, *la rubia* (the blonde) from the train...she was just here too. She came to make sure you found the place."

I'm pretty sure my jaw dropped to the sidewalk while my eyes popped out of my head. The girl from the train who had looked at the address for the blink of an eye must have gotten off at the next stop and came back to make sure that I made it. With the 79/97 taxi confusion, I had missed her, and she obviously had somewhere else to be. Even before I had gotten off the train, I remember thinking how great it was that there were still kind people in this world. But knowing that this stranger on a train cared enough to come look for me took it to a whole new level. *Increíble.* I still get goosebumps just thinking about it. I just wish she was still there when I got to Biggie's place; I could have given her something nice as a "gracias" for checking up on me...something like chocolate or vitamins or my extra packet of wet wipes because, well, you never know.

Lynn Bilbrey, a native of Puyallup, Washington, teaches in Frankfurt, Germany. She has taught middle school English and design for 15 years, 4 in the US and 11 in South Korea and Germany.

ONE THING LEADS TO ANOTHER
Matt Minor

"Four Cuba Libres, please."

Traveling alone for the first time can make a guy nervous. So can waiting for strangers at a beachside bar 8,000 miles from home.

We had just met two hours earlier on a boat ride over to the sweaty island of Boracay in the Philippines. Sardined in with the many other sunburned foreigners, we kept ourselves distracted with small talk. Smiling politely, a 20-something female introduced herself and her two companions in broken English as vacationers from China.

"I am Zhu. We comes for relaxing. It not working. Ready for beach."

With sun-faded speakers pumping out Bob Marley tunes, I eyed the four strong cocktails as they were delivered to the table. Although my new acquaintances had yet to arrive to the bar, I was certain that the "4 for 1" happy hour special would be a welcomed greeting.

The smell of buttered prawns wafted over to the table just as Zhu and her friends tiptoed through the bleached white sand. She had changed out of her city attire in favor of white shorts spotted with little green palm trees, a white tank top, and a giant grin that showed her relief to be away from the overcrowded streets of Shanghai. On the contrary, her two traveling companions were covered from head to toe in sun-protective cotton garbs and oversized visors. Picture mummies arriving to a luau.

"*Nǐ hǎo*," I said with a proud smile, having learned the Mandarin greeting years earlier. "Is anyone thirsty?"

Her friends declined the awaiting cocktails in favor of fruit juice while Zhu eagerly accepted. Before I could sit back down she took two desperate gulps, clearly parched from the long travel day. As we all settled into our sandy beach chairs, our English conversation appeared to make Zhu's friends uneasy. They shyly held hands and clung together like overcooked spaghetti. After finishing their fruit juice, Zhu's travel mates crafted their escape. They half-bowed in my direction and made their way towards the winding shoreline, relieved to exit a conversation they couldn't keep up with.

Undeterred by the language difficulties, Zhu told me all about her conservative Chinese family, her role as the black sheep within it, and the stressful engineering job she had recently begun. Painting a picture of her husband, I learned of a loving, yet unadventurous person. The kind of guy who would fund a trip, but never find the courage to experience its life-changing effects. An interested audience to her future island slideshow, but judgmental of her new temporary beach tattoo. I sensed that their differences went beyond just travel.

"These first two drinks went down like water," I said.
"I am happy for drinking more," she declared.

With a second round on the way, I shared the story of how I moved away from the comforts of family and friends, quit my secure teaching job for a riskier one in Asia, and started exploring the world. The conversation was flowing as smoothly as the rum n' cokes.

"I am wishing to confess something very important," she suddenly said.

Sensing Zhu was now feeling honest from the drink buzz, I expected to hear that this subdued rebel preferred my adventurous ways to her husband's. I began to imagine the story I would tell buddies back home of my ability to charm women across international waters.

"I am Bahá'í," she said very innocently.

Having grown up in Chicago I knew of the Bahá'í Temple, a massive domed structure with nine intricate towers that we visited during my senior year in high school. I now wished that I had paid more attention during World Religions class.

"Tell me more about your religion," I asked, secretly embarrassed that I misread the situation. "Three most important thing for me is to always be having daily prayer, never to be having food during daytime in March, and never, ever to be having alcohols," she stated just before taking the final satisfying swill of her rum drink.

"Wait, you what? Did you just say you never drink alcohol?" I asked, praying to a non-Bahá'í god for forgiveness.

"Yes, to have alcohols is very bad for Bahá'í persons!"

Had I not already been sunburned, surely she would have seen me blushing.

Zhu then exhaled a deep sigh and proclaimed, "I feels so so good now. I am relaxing and feels like beach girl. It long time since I feels so so free."

This left me to analyze whether Zhu and her anti-social friends knew what she was up to, or whether I had just corrupted a perfectly devout Bahá'í girl. I decided to do a bit of interrogation.

"You have definitely had an alcoholic drink though, right?"
"No, never."
"Do you have Bahá'í friends who follow less strict drinking rules?"
"No, none."
"But you would break the rules for a really special occasion, right?"
"No, never never!" she answered suddenly very sober.

Almost as if he had been watching the spectacle unfold, our recently inattentive waiter noticed our empty glasses and asked whether we would like a third round. As I considered confessing to Zhu that the four drinks she had already consumed had "alcohols" in them, a little voice in my head urged me to let this beach girl enjoy life for a while. Sweat trickled down my neck and back as I nervously picked at the skin around my fingernails. Avoiding eye contact with Zhu, I hoped she would make the decision for both of us and save my troubled soul.

"Do you wants more Matt?" she asked.
"Well, I...um...I think...um..."

With her fate in my hands and my morals nearly evaporated, I did what any self-respecting non-Bahá'í person would do. I faked a stomach cramp, paid the bill, and disappeared into the sunset embarrassed that tomorrow's hangover would surely tell Zhu what I couldn't.

Matt Minor, a native of Chicago (Elgin), Illinois, teaches in Medellín, Colombia. He has taught in elementary schools for 17 years, 8 in the US and 9 in South Korea, Thailand, and Colombia.

DON'T JUDGE A BOOK
Karen Taylor

Being single was not going to hold me back from my desire to travel. I had never traveled by myself, but I figured that this would be a great opportunity to see a new continent. My friend was teaching in Uganda and I planned to meet her there and then head off to Tanzania and Kenya for a safari on my own. Although none of my friends wanted or could afford to join me on a safari in Africa, I was going to go alone.

The company which arranged my first safari in Kenya arranged for a bus to take me to the second safari in Tanzania. I said goodbye to the guide, chef, and driver of my Kenyan safari and stepped on the bus. I was again adventuring alone. For the next 15 hours I slept and read as the plains of Kenya eventually transformed into the base of Kilimanjaro. I was excited to be seeing new sights and adventuring on my own. I thought myself so brave! None of my friends would ever believe it when I got back and told them what amazing sights I had seen solo!

I arrived at the bus stop in Arusha, Tanzania at 10:30 p.m. on Christmas Eve. I looked around for the company shuttle that was booked to pick me up, but after all the other passengers were greeted and the terminal emptied out, I had the sobering thought that no one may be coming for me. I waited for a while longer, hoping that the shuttle should be there any minute. Any minute. Any minute. But no one arrived. Suddenly, the reality of traveling alone became frighteningly clear.

Across the street there was a fancy hotel, but there was "no room at the inn" on Christmas Eve. The receptionist was kind enough to let me use the hotel phone to call the safari company. No answer; it was after office hours. Since the hotel probably wouldn't look too kindly upon me sleeping on the lobby floor, I walked back to the bus stop thinking, "How was I going to get through this night?"

I walked around, trying to figure out what to do next and, more importantly, trying not to look lost. Suddenly, a man approached me and asked me if I was lost. "I'm fine," I replied, lying through my grimace. I had to find a way to get out of that parking lot. Thoughts swirled through my head—Would my family ever know where I went missing? How long would it be before anyone found out where I ended up? Would anyone hear if I screamed right now at the top of my lungs?

He quickly explained, "I was your bus driver. It's my job to make sure that all of my passengers are safe. Are you OK?"

What a relief! My self-image as a brave solo female traveler had been shattered, but the pieces on the ground didn't matter. I was safe.

Just minutes away from Christmas Day, I followed my bus driver Mwamba and his co-worker Andwele up the cliffs and we approached a small house. He pointed at the door and said, "I'm sure that you are used to better, but it is a room for $2 a night. Get settled and I'll come back and check on you in a bit. In the morning I'll walk you back down to the bus stop and we'll make sure you get picked up by your safari company."

As I looked in, suspiciously expecting to see the equivalent of a $2 room in the States, I saw a queen-sized bed with fresh white sheets, a bathroom with a shower and hot water, and even curtains on the windows and a little rug on the floor. Back home, friends would have scoffed at these terribly basic accommodations with no TV or other modern necessities. But what more than a room with a door and a roof did a person really need? I was thrilled to have this place and needed nothing else. Safe and sound in my own room after such a long journey—it was perfect!

After I settled in, Mwamba and Andwele returned to take me to a fried chicken restaurant where we ate, drank, and laughed at my follies. I apologized for being scared and stressed and was so happy to spend time with these men who had been my saviors. Together we sampled the local beer and disputed which type of fried chicken was the best. Mwamba lent me his phone to call the safari company; I noticed that Jesus was his screensaver. Another reason to breathe easier, I thought to myself. It was so delightful to share food and drink with these men, who had become my heroes and knights in bus uniforms.

The next morning, promptly at our pre-arranged time, Mwamba and Andwele came to the door to walk me back to the bus station. I thanked them again for their help and told them how grateful I was. They responded with humility, "we are just doing our jobs, nothing more." I got onto my new bus and waved goodbye to these humble and honest men.

I have often taught my students the proverb, "Don't judge a book by its cover." Despite hearing and teaching it many times, I still needed to learn it, myself. There, while traveling by myself in a foreign country, I realized that the world truly is made up of good people who are willing to help others. Whether my future travels are with others or by myself, trust in humanity is something I will always pack in my bag.

Karen Taylor, a native of San Jose, California, teaches in Sacramento, California. She has taught middle and high school English for 15 years, 6 in the US and 9 in the Philippines, South Korea, Bolivia, and Colombia.

MONKEY SEE
Jay Goodman

Only our faces and hands remain exposed, and even the
exposed skin isn't really exposed; it's covered in a thick layer of
sunscreen and bug cream, giving everyone a sort of post-
Thriller Michael Jacksonish look. My colleague Dale, an Iowa
kid born of the sort of Dutch heritage that produces
reasonable high-school athletes, is khakied-up, boots to hat,
and is squinting into the sun. "It's hot here," he says. His shirt
is already sticking to his chest.

The Amazon River this time of year is flooded. Two hundred
feet back from the normal shoreline is now under thirteen feet
of water. Some houses are built as rafts; as the water rises, so
does the house. Others are built on stilts, and some families
simply sacrifice their lower levels for four or five months a
year. I had no idea where we'd be staying; hopefully it wasn't
the house with the family eating on the roof as though they

tired of waiting for the rescue helicopter and decided, well, I guess this is just how we live now.

One of the bizarre things about teaching internationally is how your colleagues become your assigned friends, travel companions, and occasional lovers. They're also the people who you look at when departing into the Amazon and think, I wonder which one of these eleven people will be the first to perish, will I eat them, and what part of the human body goes best with river catfish. I was sure it would be Dale. Though a perfectly competent human being in many areas of his life, Dale had spent the last three weeks asking questions about mosquitos, heat, and what kind of clothing offered the best protection against both (and punctuating each piece of information he received with a shake of the head and a "Oh gosh"). He settled on rubber boots, knee high socks, zip-off pants, a brownish-grey button-up, a green poncho, and a hat that came with a snap-on neck flap ("My mom told me to protect my neck." "You're mixing up your mom with Wu-Tang again." "What do you mean?") and a string to tighten it under his chin, which he removed because he said it made him look stupid. He also carried a dull hunting knife for protection against jaguars.

Our vehicle for the trip was a long 200-horsepower covered river boat that drew about a foot of water. But it wasn't agile enough to navigate the flooded walking path to our first night's accommodations, so we transferred to canoes. I sat in the front, hoping for the best view as we floated between 400-year-old trees, Tarzan vines and fruits so exotic that they're unknown to anyone outside the banks of the river. Then the guide told me to turn around, and I realized I was now in the stern of the canoe, staring at the back of the heads of two Colombians who I didn't know, who didn't speak English, and who viewed my weak Spanish as a mental deficiency. They explained to me that the trees grow because of water and that seeds are from fruit and that there are many fish in the river. I pretended not to understand anything, and eventually they stopped talking to me, except to sometimes turn, make brief eye contact with me, and then laugh with the guide seated behind me. I spent the rest of the two-hour paddle scooping leaves from the water and lobbing them at Dale four seats up. A combination of wind, bad aim, and a neck flap prevented him from ever noticing.

The guide told us that there's this fish in the Amazon that feeds on nitrates emitted from the gills of some other fish. Whatever this chemical is, human urine contains the same chemical, and so peeing in the river presents a horrifying danger. If you pee in the river, this tiny fish will swim up the urine stream and jam itself in your urethra. Fear of the urethra shark cut our swim-time short that afternoon, which prompted us to return to a small town early and see if we could find some beers. That was when we lost Dale. The town has two roads, both for foot traffic only, and so it seems difficult that we could have lost a 6'2" Steve Irwin in such a short period of time. While none of us were overly concerned, our guide, whose livelihood is tied pretty closely to not losing Gringos in the middle of the Amazon, was extremely disturbed. He hatched a rescue plan. He found a seven-year-old kid named Pablo wandering around the village, gave him a description of Dale, and sent him off. Pablo went fifteen feet, stopped the first white person he saw, a 65-year-old greybeard, and asked if he was Dale. If this kid was our lead detective, Dale was gone for good.

But about an hour later we found Dale sitting alone at a bar, hidden under his poncho, drinking a beer, and watching the kids swim on their flooded basketball court.
"Dale, we've been looking for you for over an hour," I told him.
"Oh. How come?"
"Because you were lost. In the middle of the Amazon."

"No, I've been right here. Watch this kid do a backflip off the rim. He's amazing."

"Dale, you can't wander off in the Amazon. There are anacondas and caimans and poison frogs everywhere."

He shrugged. "Yeah, but not here."

It was a good point. And so we joined him. Two hours later our detective found us. He was panting, drenched in sweat and wet up to his waist. He reported to Dale that he had searched the town several times and hadn't found Dale anywhere. Dale, unbothered by not knowing who this was or what he was saying, tipped him handsomely.

Our home that night was also the home of a monkey whisperer. Early afternoon we all boarded our 16-person canoe for our monkey-spotting adventure. We had no idea where we were going, and I imagined us deep in the jungle infiltrating some Jane Goodall monkey community. Instead we paddled the width of the lake, about ten meters, and drove the nose of the canoe into the bushes. Then the guide gave us all a banana. We waited. Nothing happened. He pulled out more bananas and then slammed his paddle against the hull of the boat. The monkeys emerged. They came for the bananas and also came for Dale. The first monkey crawled up and down him like a branch, unconcerned that this tree was squirming and squealing. It grabbed the banana in chunks twice the size of its hand and tried to jam them in its mouth. A piece fell into the plastic bag that Dale was (inexplicably) carrying his camera in. The monkey and Dale both lost their shit. It grabbed at the bag, ripping and chewing at the plastic, kicking at Dale's chest. Dale hollered and swatted and thrashed about without the sort of caution someone in a canoe surrounded by alligators and piranhas usually exhibits. The commotion drew a second monkey, who didn't seem interested in the camera or banana, but was interested in trying to crawl through the buttons of Dale's shirt. "Help, it's going to go in my shirt and then try to get out my arm and then get stuck and then I'm going to have a monkey in my shirt!" he yelled, which despite his obvious panic, was a very accurate description of a thing that could happen. That didn't happen, though. The camera monkey was now on Dale's shoulder, hanging to one side, eating the bit of banana he retrieved through the hole in the plastic bag. The other monkey, sensing an opportunity, jumped onto Dale's upper arm, grabbed the first monkey by his tiny exposed penis, and began to fellate him. Dale didn't notice, and no one who did could get a word out through their own excitement. Only one person maintained composure and managed to capture what will certainly become a legendary tale and framed photo for generations of Dales: "Has your grandfather ever told you about the time he was involved in a monkey threesome? No? Dale, show them the picture."

Somehow, Dale didn't die that trip. But were it not for the miracle of modern medicine, I would have. Three weeks after we got back to Medellin, I was standing in front of my class when I felt the need to lean against the desk. A moment later I said "Guys, I feel a bit off, I'll be back in a minute." But minutes can get away from you, and within a couple of hours I was lying in a hospital, tied to my bed with an IV, covered by a mesh net, listening to a doctor tell me a bunch of things, of which I only understood a single word. Malaria. I breathed in deeply, closed my eyes, and thought about how the only thing worse than having malaria was knowing that Dale didn't.

Jay Goodman, a native of Toronto, Ontario, teaches in Dalian, China. He has taught high school English school for 10 years, 4 in Canada and 6 in Honduras, Colombia, and China.

VI. LEAVING OVERSEAS

A GIFT OF LIFE FROM BOTH SIDES
Christine Martin

I've looked at life from both sides now
From win and lose and still somehow
It's life's illusions I recall
I really don't know life at all — *Joni Mitchell*

Sitting at a local café in my California neighborhood, I am attuned to the conversations around me—two women discussing their last yoga class, a father convincing his toddler to pet the dog, and the cafe owner bantering with regulars. My memory flipped to a time, when I lived in other countries, where conversations around me were like white noise…fuzzy and unintelligible. There are times when I miss that.

After paying for my coffee, I settled down to write about my life teaching overseas. For weeks in preparation, I invited my memories in; I jotted down details from the cities in which I lived and the travel experiences which had the most impact. I have quite a list of stories to choose from—11 years' worth to be exact.

But I realized that this essay request is very challenging for me. As in the lyrics above, I now see both sides of international living: the exit from my overseas career, and the re-entry to my home country.

Four years ago, I made one of the toughest decisions of my life. I decided to come back home to California, after many years teaching overseas. While it was expected, I didn't realize the transition would be harder than my many relocations to foreign countries because of culture shock. Culture shock can hit you when you least expect it. It can happen when you find yourself overwhelmed while standing in a row of condiments at a Safeway supermarket or after the shock of receiving a medical bill of $550 for blood tests. It can happen while attempting, unsuccessfully, to plan time to spend with friends or feeling unsafe during and after a presidential election. All are difficult to understand.

Before I left for my first overseas position, I had a good life back in California, with a job I loved, a community that supported me, and an environment I admired. The impetus for leaving was a combination of opportunity and a broken heart. I told myself that I would only go to Medellin for one year and get it out of my system; then I would come back home.

But, while the intention was to spend a year learning and healing, it actually led to a decade of exploration and growth. I had completely fallen for a new way of life. I relished leafing through my passport to review its stamps and visas. At first, I wrote long detailed emails and, later, became inspired to write a blog where I recounted my adventures as well as quotidian events. My photos told a story of this exciting life that I had come to love, a life that included scuba diving, dancing tango in Colombia, trekking the Sahara on a camel, spending long weekends in Nice, and doing yoga in Bali. After the 3rd year, my family and friends stopped asking when I would return; in fact, I wasn't so sure I would.

There was a revelatory moment, on the beach at Negros in the Philippines, on a Spring Break vacation, when my friends and I realized how grateful we were to have found the key that opened this world to us. We were financially comfortable, enjoyed our work, and got to travel.

However, all good things have a price. Leaving home each time was always hard. Saying good-bye to my aging parents made me incredibly sad. I was uncomfortable and had a 'fear of missing out' (FOMO) on big life events, like weddings and births. I wasn't living the life of a typical American. I didn't have kids or a mortgage or debt or a measly two week summer vacation. I pondered whether I was taking the easy road without real responsibilities. Was it fair to be happy while others were suffering from lack of funds or lack of time? I realized that guilt had gripped me.

Nevertheless, living overseas challenged me in many ways. While my friends and I enjoyed the luxury of debating where to spend our next vacation and how to tuck money away into savings, my apartment was not my real home. The friendships, which felt like family, were really not. The feeling was always that you were from someplace else. I developed an identity crisis because my heart was in both the place I grew up and also in the place where I lived.

The time finally arrived to return home.

My Marco Polo app notifies me when a new video of a friend is available for view. For a moment, I am connected with Jenn on the beach in Ko Samui or I'm sharing Sara's camping holiday in New Zealand. Seeing snippets of the life I gave up is both inspiring and painful. While I have experienced growth, success, and love upon my return home, I do miss my old life.

I hear nostalgia, torment, and tenderness in Joni Mitchell's words; I understand. Seeing life from both sides is both beautiful and painful, but I now know that it is a gift.

Christine Martin lives in California. You may remember her from such stories as "A Trilogy of the Best Kept Secrets."

CONCLUSION

WRAPPING IT UP
Kevin A. Duncan

The earth has journeyed around the sun once and already started another orbit since Matty O'Minor and I were "talking smart" on that balcony in Colombia. During that time, talk of a book went from a fanciful dream to a reality. Starting with friends, then moving to friends of friends, and then expanding even further afield, we've felt fortunate to have so many people, thirty-five to be exact (living in eighteen different countries), contribute stories from Turkey to Thailand, Morocco to Mexico and beyond.

While collecting stories, editing, and doing other book-related tasks, we've continued to experience the rollercoaster ride that is international teaching. Nine months after spending my Chinese New Year break flying from Guangzhou to Medellin to visit two of my closest friends—Matt and his wife Cailin—I landed a job at an international school in Buenos Aires for the upcoming school year. Finally, after 5 years on different continents, I would be living near the Minors again! Two weeks later, Matt and Cailin accepted jobs teaching in Shanghai for the next school year, only a mere two-hour flight from my current home in Guangzhou. Ouch. So much for the reunion.

On a positive note, I'll be able to reconnect in South America with former colleagues from my China and Korea days while Matt and Cailin will get to live in a city with friends they met in Korea, Colombia, and the US. In the meantime, we'll make the most of our final weeks in our respective schools and countries, perhaps squeezing too much into a short amount of time as the process of procuring visas, downsizing, packing, crossing off bucket list items, and saying goodbyes compete with our professional responsibilities. Preparing to move to yet another country and school where we've never visited is now par for the course. This isn't unusual anymore. It's our new normal.

WEBSITES

Please remember that 100% of all proceeds from this book will go to support educating students via the Children of Haiti Project. To further donate or to learn more, please go to http://www.childrenofhaitiproject.org/.

To find author bios, pictures that go with some of the stories, information on how to share a story for a possible 2nd edition, and more, check out this book's website at http://thenewnormalbook.weebly.com/.

THANK YOUS

FROM MATT:

A special thanks to Dunc for pushing me out of my comfort zone and for challenging me at a time when I needed it most.

To my wife Cailin, for always finding the perfect balance of criticism, honesty, and love when giving feedback about my story and on the revisions for this book.

To my mom Sandy, for always giving me the gift of her time, both when I was a fumbling 10 year-old writer and now as a 39 year-old author who has the confidence to rant to whomever will listen.

To my dad Bob, for his constant encouragement to follow my dreams, whether that be my pursuit to become a professional baseball player (spoiler alert: I didn't make it!) or my decision to move thousands of miles from home to reinvent myself.

To my brother Mikey, for spending countless hours "talking smart" with me across continents and in person whenever I am home.

FROM KEVIN:

A huge gracias to Matt for the truly meaningful friendship, great example in so many phases of life, and consistently amusing voice messages this past year.

To Myra Thomas and Dave Archer, people I've known at quite different times in my life, for inspiring me to share my stories with others.

To my many teachers, from preschool to grad school, that truly cared about me as both a student and person.

To my family in Tennessee—I am incredibly lucky to be a Duncan. Most significantly, to my parents Tom and Judy for the unbelievable amount of support you have given me throughout the years. Your love for life and education hopefully shine through me as I continuously try to grow as a teacher and person.

FROM BOTH OF US:
To Bambi Betts, for trusting our idea and connecting us with the people and resources to help make this book happen. When we approached her with this book/fundraising idea a few months ago she quickly connected us to a vast network of administrators and teachers all over the world.

To Ettie Zilber and Linda Mishkin, for volunteering their time to help a group of teachers become published authors writing for a common cause.

To Soren Sturlaugson, for sketching and designing our book cover. We feel very lucky to have had an international teacher and talented artist share his talents with us in order to bring our stories to life on the cover.

To Sofia Restrepo, a skilled grade 12 student who donated her photoshop talents and keen eye for design to this project. Her collaboration with Soren turned a drawing into a legit book cover.

To Juan Felipe Gaviria and Camila Vélez, both international school students, for volunteering to create our website and helping to raise awareness for the COHP.

Finally, to all of the teachers who took a risk, submitted a story, and are now published authors. Without you this book would have remained only a dream. Thank you for entertaining, enlightening, and giving back to international education.

Made in the USA
Middletown, DE
30 April 2017